Liberty
Reflections of an Oklahoma Glass Company and its Family

Liberty

Reflections of an Oklahoma Glass Company and its Family

by Rebecca Dixon
Foreword by Fulton Collins IV

Sapulpa Historical Society & Museum
100 E. Lee Avenue,
Sapulpa, OK 74066
(p) 918-224-4871
(f) 918-224-7765
sapulpahistsoc@tulsacoxmail.com

2014 Board of Directors

President
Rick Woolery

Vice President
Larry White

Secretary
Belinda Crosby

Treasurer
Russell Crosby

Board Members

Carolyn Bartlett
Maryetta Collins
Chief Eaton
Ron Gibson
Frank Gierhart
Dick Hermes
Mike Jeffries
Caroll Jobe
Bob Langston
Darla Reed
Joe Sherwood
Sherry Sherwood
Lloyd Skinner
Sue Skinner
Dan Whitehouse

Copyright 2014 by Sapulpa Historical Society & Museum.

All rights reserved. No part of this book may be produced or utilized in any form or by any means, electronic or mechanical, including photocopying and recording, by any information storage and retrieval system, without permission of the publisher, the Sapulpa Historical Society & Museum and the Collins Family.

Printed in Canada.
ISBN: 978-0-615-95594-0

Designed by Brean Crosby Fowler

LG

Liberty

Reflections of an Oklahoma Glass Company and its Family

Foreword .... *iii*

Chapter 1 - The Legacy of the Liberty Glass Company *1*

Chapter 2 - The First Family of Liberty Glass ~ Part 1 .... *12*

Chapter 3 - I Am Glass - The Liberty Glass Story *16*

Chapter 4 - The First Family of Liberty Glass ~ Part 2 .... *34*

Chapter 5 - If Only These Walls Could Talk, Inside the Liberty Glass Plant *52*

Chapter 6 - The First Family of Liberty Glass ~ Part 3 .... *70*

Chapter 7 - The Departments of Liberty Glass *78*

Chapter 8 - The Strike of 1983 .... *96*

Chapter 9 - The Turnaround *108*

Chapter 10 - Fulton's Finest Hour *112*

Chapter 11 - The Legacy Left Behind... .... *120*

Addendum 1 - Tulsa - Sapulpa Union Railway & Red Ball Trucking *132*

Addendum 2 - The Collins Building *150*

Acknowledgements *156*

Foreword
By Fulton Collins IV

September 2013, nearly 20 years since my father sold our family business, the Liberty Glass Company, and I still have a 6 ½ ounce contour Coca-Cola bottle manufactured by LG sitting on my desk. The bottle is a reminder of so many things for me, but more importantly a symbol of a company and the family that ran it for almost 80 years.

I still remember the first time I toured the plant over four decades ago. The Liberty Glass plant was American red, white and blue-collar manufacturing through and through, which was represented not only in its name, but by the team of people who worked there.

For a young boy, the plant was a fascinating place to visit–a compelling wonderland in some ways, and yet dangerous and scary in others. Motion everywhere is how a visitor was greeted upon entry–raw materials being carted by conveyors, lifts and cranes, batched together in precise amounts to create the formula for high-quality glass containers. The gas furnace, heating the mixture at over 2000 degrees Fahrenheit, was visually passive and at the same time sensationally intense. Just beyond the furnace lay the excitement of the bottle manufacturing extravaganza. Hot molten gobs of glass would emerge from supply pipes overhead, almost as if they were being born. They literally pulsed with colors of fiery orange and red, leaving the casual observer to feel that they were alive. As they emerged from the molds, they would gradually cool and turn into a pristine sparkling bottle with the purity of a perfect gem. Of course not everything was perfect every time, but therein lay some of the excitement of the experience. It was really a wonderful process to watch.

For most of us very little thought goes into the consumption of a soda. The pop of the cap, the lift to the mouth, the cool sensation of the container against our lips, sweetness on our tongue and refreshment down our throat–a simple activity recreated every day all over the world. Few of us ever think much beyond that, but that is the interesting thing about consumer products–the experience is so much more than just the product–it is the entire package. You could put any brown liquid in a Coke bottle, and people will think it's a Coke because of the bottle. For some, it is not a Coke unless it's in a Coke bottle.

My great grandfather started Liberty Glass in 1918. It would be part of our family for close to eight decades, and it played a big part not just in our lives, but the people who worked there formed an equally strong bond with Liberty, as we generally referred to it. I never met my great grandfather, as he passed before I was born, leaving the company to his two children, my Grandpa George and my Great Aunt Loreine. My memories of both of them are interwoven with memories of Liberty Glass. I remember visiting my grandfather's office in the Collins Building, seeing countless glass bottles for products I had never seen before, names like Rebel Soda and Grapette, which were perhaps common to some, seemed like a candy store of beverages to me. It was "cool" to say the least, and it is also where the glass bottle on my desk came from.

However, my memories of Liberty then were of an archetypal classic time, and less of a company that would come to be recognized as one of the best in the world in its industry. I remember visiting Liberty shortly after my Uncle Roger had implemented changes in the technologies being used to operate the business, and for me that was in many ways the inflection point from being this neat company my grandfather ran to being a company that was positioning for a new era of manufacturing. It was a period in which Liberty really flourished, and a period in which my father and Jim Bolin were able to collaborate and say "what if."

Following my grandfather's passing my dad moved back to Tulsa to work on both the estate and the company. In a fortunate way my grandfather's passing saved the company, because it brought my father back to Liberty to operate and invest in the business in a way that had never been done before. I can vividly recall Dad saying, "We are going to do one thing, and we are going to do it better than anyone else." It was a challenging time for many, as Liberty went through a transformation of epic proportions, but it positioned the company to be able to succeed in an industry that had changed from small individual businesses to manufacturing conglomerates operating on a global scale.

Even as Liberty thrived and innovated, it still remained a small independent player that was dwarfed by its primary competitors. The passion of its employees, especially Jim Bolin, played a huge part in its ability to compete, but the main driver was the Collins family, specifically my father's willingness to invest in a changing industry so Liberty Glass could compete. Now that Dad is gone, I can only speculate that in some ways that he felt a duty to see it through. It was a challenge to succeed and take Liberty as part of the Collins family as far as he could within the limitations of the industry's reality.

When the opportunity to sell the company came along, I recall Dad saying that business should not be emotional, and for the most part I think he believed that, but Liberty Glass was not just a business, it was part of the family. It had been around for four generations of Collins. It was a place that many family members had worked their entire professional careers.

Like many things in life, absence makes the heart grow fonder. There are so many memories for the Collins family at Liberty Glass, and it will forever be part of our history –one that is simply symbolized by a Coke bottle on my desk.

"POP"…..ahh.

AMBASSADORS
of Good Will and Good Health

Chapter One

1918 — 1994

The legacy of the
Liberty Glass Company

Liberty...it was a name born out of patriotism. Throughout the years there ran a common thread, an unbroken theme of Freedom and American pride, of hard work and hopeful optimism. These were the standards upon which Liberty Glass was founded and the standards that remained when the company closed its doors seventy-six years later.

This is the story of a plant and its people and the legacy left behind.

Based in Sapulpa, Oklahoma, Liberty made its mark in glass manufacturing by specializing in returnable containers for the dairy and soda industries. Other glass items produced by Liberty over the years included medicine bottles, beer, wine and liquor bottles as well as a general line of food containers. A company slogan for Liberty was "See what you buy—buy in glass."

Founded by George Collins Sr. in 1918, Liberty remained in the Collins family for three generations. Following George Sr. as CEO was George Jr., who took over the company in 1939, and George III or Fulton, as he was known, who ran Liberty from 1980 until the sale of the plant in 1994.

During its lifetime, Liberty Glass was successful and well respected, especially in the local community.

Carolyn "Kitty" Hunt
Secretary to George F. Collins Jr.
1967-1980

"If you said, 'I'm with Liberty', that carried some clout."

Ted Fisher
Sapulpa Community Leader
Majority Leader Oklahoma State Senate

"I wasn't here very long before we got to know the human capital that Liberty brought to Sapulpa. I'm talking about stellar, stellar assets to the community. Their employment base was certainly important to the community."

"Being with Montgomery Ward, I started selling to people who worked at Liberty Glass and easily discerned the impact that company brought to our community. I got to know very quickly they were one valuable corporate citizen."

"All great companies are so because of their people, and they had a knack for hiring good people."

MANUFACTURERS OF
HIGH GRADE MILK BOTTLES

Mike Tyler
Former Oklahoma House of Representatives District 30
Sapulpa Community Leader and Businessman

"The working-class at Liberty was our mainstay. We had so many of their employees who traded with us. When refrigerators came out with shelves in the doors, we didn't put plastic bottles in those refrigerators. We put GLASS bottles in them because they were on display. Things like that we were very conscious of because we cared about the people like they cared about us."

"They were very, very community involved. I keep going back to my business because they helped keep us alive. The business even traded with us. If they needed a refrigerator they didn't buy out of town. They traded local. We appreciated that, and they helped keep us there for so many years."

Frank Gierhart
Sapulpa Business and Community Leader
Gabe's Printing

"They kept us alive. We didn't go through a day that we didn't do something for Liberty Glass and they were good friends."

"People who worked there were all over the town, and they were a major, major part of Sapulpa."

Judge Rick Woolery
Judge of District Court
Sapulpa Community Leader
President, Sapulpa Historical Museum

"I always read the newspaper, every word in it, and I remember that several times a year Liberty had full-page ads. It seems like Labor Day was a big time for an ad for them and they usually had a full-page ad for the Christmas season. I remember thinking how nice it was that they would do that. Sometimes they would thank their employees or list their employees."

David Block
IT Department Manager
1967-1994

"Liberty Glass was the primary employer in Sapulpa. They provided people with a good working environment and they also paid the best wages. Liberty was a really great place to work. It was a lot of fun and it was a great environment. The people were really great."

The Legacy of the Liberty Glass Company

Most would agree it was the people who made Liberty special, people who put in a solid day's work no matter what hardships and problems they might be facing outside the plant. Liberty was a good job and a well-paying one, but for the workers there were often too many bills to pay and too many babies to feed.

During the 1930's, the Depression and Dust Bowl both took a toll on Oklahoma. All across the state people were hurting, and the men and women of Liberty were no exception.

On a broader front, two World Wars, the Cold War and later Vietnam shook the company to its core. Men were called to serve and families suffered, not knowing what the future might hold. But this was a company founded on the principles of patriotism, and if freedom meant putting up a fight, then that's what they would do.

On June 9, 1944, the Sapulpa Herald announced the formation of the "Liberty Liberators" at the Liberty Glass Company. This was a group of over 300 men and women who joined together so they could exceed their quota of war bonds. They wanted to build more Liberator Bombers to help the 118 men who represented the company in the war.

Jackie Rule Robertson
Accounting Department
1942-1943

"Of course, everybody was in it together. Everybody was working for a purpose then."

"Women were going to work, because the men were leaving."

Even during the difficult times at Liberty, there remained things trouble couldn't touch. Friendships were formed at the company, friendships that would sometimes last a lifetime.

> Linda Campbell
> Sales Department Receptionist
>
> *"I think there was good communication among all departments, and good friendships that have lasted. I mean look how long we've all been gone from Liberty Glass, and we still call each other and check on each other."*

Linda Campbell's supervisor at Liberty, Wills Young, started a new business after Liberty sold, and the first person he hired was Linda. Today the two are still great friends and continue to work together at Wills' company.

Velma Littlefield and Catherine Williams were employed together in the Packing Department at the plant. Velma started in 1955 and Catherine came three years later. The two were immediately drawn to each other and Velma said she ended up with a friend for life in Catherine.

> Velma Littlefield
> Packing/Lab/ Box Shop/Label Machine
> 1955-1996
>
> *"She had worked a while and they put us together. I don't know, for some reason we just got along. She just put up with me, and we stayed pretty well together until I went to the lab. We've just remained friends ever since."*

Together the two women worked a total of 67 years at the plant, and today their friendship continues. Catherine now has trouble with her vision and can't drive, so Velma takes her wherever she needs to go.

The Legacy of the Liberty Glass Company

Throughout the years new friends were found at Liberty, but old friendships also played a part in company culture. High School classmates worked side by side at the plant. People whose families had known each other for years—families who had gone to church together, and who laughed and played together, often found themselves forging yet another bond, this time at work. David Block and David Feiker, two teammates from Sapulpa's high school basketball squad, teamed up again in the 1970's, this time to lead Liberty's IT Department. Old and new friends made Liberty all the more special.

David Feiker
IT Department Programmer/Systems Analyst
1976-1994

"We worked together and we were fortunate. We'd go out to eat, we'd go do things and our families would do things. It was a good company."

Margaret A. Fuller
Sales Department
1968-74
Plant Manager Secretary
1976-77

"It was a great job. I knew everyone and everyone knew me."

Ted Fisher
Sapulpa Community Leader
Majority Leader Oklahoma State Senate

"Hardly anybody we talked to in our age group who grew up here didn't work at Liberty at one time or another."

Joyce Steavenson
Secretary to the Treasurer
1951-1958

"We really did have a good time at the office. We got our work done, but we still had fun."

"Liberty was fun, it really was."

Mold Shop Supervisor Bill Oldham started at Liberty in 1956 when he was only 19. He stayed for 44 years, and today still loves talking about his time at the plant.

Bill Oldham
Mold-Maker/Mold Shop Supervisor
1956-1994

"We laughed and fought and argued and everything else, but we considered ourselves pretty much a family."

To most employees, their friends at Liberty did seem like family, and sometimes they actually were.

Terry Kelly
Director of Purchasing/Manager of Engineering Services
1965-1994

"You've got people out there who their grandfather, father and son worked out there."

The Oldhams were one such family. Bill Oldham was a second generation Liberty man, preceded by his father Frank, the first in the family to work at the plant. Bill was followed by his two sons, who made up the third generation at Liberty, and Bill remembers that the only advice he gave his boys was to do whatever their supervisor told them to do.

David Feiker, who came to the IT Department in 1976, says what he found at Liberty was the family he'd always longed to have.

David Feiker
IT Department Programmer/Systems Analyst
1976-1994

"It was family owned, and that was really important to me. I wanted to be at a company where I felt like I was going to be there for a long time. I had a pretty unstable childhood, and I wanted something stable to come to."

David Beyer
Accounting Department
Chief Financial Officer
1972-1994

"Liberty Glass was always a good company and took good care of their people. About twenty days after I started work there, I had an emergency appendectomy and I was off work for a week, and of course I wasn't covered by health insurance yet, but they continued my pay. There wasn't any question about it. They took care of me during that period. It was a family-oriented company. I didn't even ask for it, but they just continued my salary, and I had been there less than a month."

Sometimes brand new families were even formed at Liberty. Cupid came calling on a regular basis, and a number of employees met their future spouses on the job. No doubt these romantic relationships added a little spice to life at Liberty.

Tom Syrles
Shipping Manager/Traffic Manager
1966-1990

"That's actually where I met my wife. She was working in the decorating department, and I happened to meet her there."

Bob Hill
Mold Shop
1956-1994

"I met my wife Dottie out there. She was working in the cold end packing those bottles. She was working the midnight shift. Three to eleven, I think then. I met her there on the job and got a mild reprimand for visiting with the help."

Bill Oldham
Mold-Maker/Mold Shop Supervisor
1956-1994

"Mine was love at first sight."

"I got out of school the middle of June, and we were working in the decorating department washing bottles. It was probably the first week I worked there."

"When you came out of the old time clock shaft, there was a bench that sat out front by the railroad tracks. Barbara was sitting there, and it was the first time I ever saw her. She was a really pretty girl with green jeans and a green checked shirt."

"I asked her if she'd like a ride home."

Not all romances were love at first sight like Bill Oldham's. Chief Financial Officer David Beyer met his future wife Vickie in Liberty's Accounting Department in 1974, but the couple didn't actually date for another 20 years.

Vickie Varnell Beyer
Accounting Department
1974-1976, 1983-1990

"I was 17 years old, and my mother worked at Liberty. I got a summer job after I graduated high school."

"When I went back to Liberty in 1983 [after attending OSU], I was a single parent. My priorities had changed, and my goals had changed also. I was a back-to-school mom. Education and tuition were benefits Liberty offered. I took full advantage of that, and I felt it was a very generous benefit. It helped me do some things with my life that I wouldn't have been able to do otherwise."

For all those who came to Liberty Glass looking for a job, many found so much more. Today the old plant bears a new name, but for the men and women who worked there, the place is still the stuff of memories and ghosts of friends who've passed. Looming into the sky, the striking twin batch towers continue to serve as a beacon to those traveling back in time.

There are some who claim the city of Sapulpa and glass making go together like ham and eggs. The founding of Premium Glass by George F. Collins Sr. in 1912 marked the town's entry into the industry, but this was only the beginning for George Sr. and glass making in Sapulpa. Premium was later absorbed into Liberty Glass and soon after, Sapulpa would boast a total of four major glass producers.

In addition to Liberty, Bartlett-Collins, Schram and Sunflower also made glass.

Harrison "Bart" Bartlett
Great Grandson of H.U. Bartlett
(Owner of Sapulpa Gas Company/ Co-Owner Bartlett Collins Glass Company)

As told to David Beyer - Accounting Department/Chief Financial Officer   1972-1994

"George Collins Sr. owned and operated the Sunflower Glass Company. H.U. Bartlett owned the Sapulpa Gas Company. The two businessmen formed Bartlett Collins Glass Company in 1915. Plant 1 was the original Sunflower plant on Mission. Plant 2 was constructed and became known as BC. Around 1922, shortly after Ed Bartlett (H. U. Bartlett's son) returned from WWI, he and George Collins Sr. decided to split the company.

Plant 1 produced bottles and Plant 2 produced tableware. Each plant was in a different market.

Management for the two companies was split on the basis of where employees wanted to work. For example, the senior production manager was asked which plant he wanted to work, and then the second senior production manager was asked if he would go to the opposite plant.

The split was amicable, and over the ensuing years the two companies shared idle equipment, traded raw materials during shortages and shared company expertise."

The Legacy of the Liberty Glass Company

Mike Tyler
Former Oklahoma House of Representatives
District 30
Sapulpa Community Leader and
Businessman

"Our background is in glass, that's what we've been noted for forever. From Frankoma Pottery to Liberty Glass and BC [Bartlett-Collins], that was it, that's what we were noted for. We were a strong community in that way."

Judge Rick Woolery
Judge of District Court
Sapulpa Community Leader
President, Sapulpa Historical Museum

"I moved here from Oklahoma City at the start of my eighth grade year. The most surprising thing I remember is the glass milk bottles. Those weren't common in the Oklahoma City market, and I don't think I'd ever seen a glass milk bottle. In Oklahoma City we had the small plastic milk cartons at school, and at home we had the half gallon cardboard carton. Surprisingly, everybody here in Sapulpa had the big glass jug with the handle that you took back for a refund."

Mike Jeffries
Sapulpa Community Leader
Sapulpa Historical Museum Director

"I just thought everybody had glass bottles. Glass bottles were a way of life for those of us who grew up in Sapulpa."

Because of its domination in the glass industry, Sapulpa became known as "The Crystal City of the Southwest" according to the Encyclopedia of Oklahoma History. However, history tells us that was not always the case.

The area around Sapulpa mainly produced walnuts when the town was founded. Next, Sapulpa became known for its brick industry, and in 1898 the Sapulpa Pressed Brick was established, followed a few years later by the Sapulpa Brick Company. This began the town's entry into the clay products industry; however, it was not until the Glenpool oilfield was discovered a few miles away in 1905 that Sapulpa grew from a small village to a larger, more prosperous town.

Over the years, many have asked why the city proved to be such an attraction for the glass industry. The answer comes from the earth. Making quality glass requires sand of high silica content, limestone, dolomite, soda ash and feldspar. Oklahoma was blessed with most of these ingredients. It had sand from the Arbuckle area and large deposits of limestone and dolomite nearby.

Equally important, thanks to the Glenpool field, Sapulpa now had essential reserves of cheap fuel in the form of natural gas required for glass manufacturing

George F. Collins Sr. knew these facts, and that is why he brought the old Premium Glass Company from Coffeyville, Kansas, to Sapulpa in 1912. For George, it was a decision that proved to be a date with destiny.

The former farm boy from Kansas moved his family to their new Oklahoma home in a wagon. After his arrival the Creek County Republican newspaper reported that once construction began on the Premium plant, George expected to be operating within 90 days, employing about a hundred men in the business of making glass.

Six years later George organized the Liberty Glass Company, which took over the Premium plant in 1918. Little did anyone know at the time, but for George Collins and his family, the American Dream was about to unfold.

Chapter Two

The First Family of *Liberty Glass*
Part 1

Most would agree that Liberty Glass and the Collins Family are synonymous in Sapulpa. George F. Collins Sr. founded the company in 1918 and his grandson, George III, or Fulton as he was known, led Liberty at the time it was sold 76 years later. In between the two leaders, George Jr. ran the company from 1939 to 1980.

George F. Collins, Sr.

Chief Executive Officer
1918-1939

George Collins Sr. didn't set out to become a pioneer in the glass industry. It just sort of happened. He was born on a farm in Thayer, Kansas, and graduated from the high school there. He finished his education at Baker University, a Methodist-based school in Baldwin, Kansas. George went on to become a school teacher and a superintendent in Neodesha, Kansas. Next he spent two years employed on a farm in Texas, and after that George returned to Kansas, moving to Coffeyville, where he worked in the newspaper business for the Daily Journal.

Even though he enjoyed his time in journalism, it was George's next move that would define the rest of his career. That's when he became associated with his father-in-law John Weaver, who had started the Premium Glass Company in Coffeyville in 1908. This was the Collins family's first venture into an industry that would consume them for three generations over the next 70 years.

Sapulpa Herald.
Date unknown.

In the fall of 1912, George Fulton Collins Sr., from Coffeyville, Kansas moved the Premium Glass Company to a location which was then far out in the country northeast of Sapulpa.

The company was relocated after a disastrous fire in Coffeyville. Mr. Collins selected Sapulpa after receiving encouragement from the Chamber of Commerce. The big factor that influenced the location here was Oklahoma gas, and the special sand which is the main ingredient for making glassware. The geological name for this sand is the "Mississippi Sand" which is found in abundance in Oklahoma.

Sapulpa Daily Argus
September 4, 1914

Perhaps the fact that Mr. Collins is an ex-newspaper man makes him realize and appreciate the value of advertising for his wares, which are already becoming widely known through the use of printers' ink. His success with the Premium plant comes from that fact. His scholastic experience has kept him in good stead in handling young men, and there is a close association between the genial manager and his employees, no doubt due to his past training.

It is only fair to state of this citizen that he is like his associates, very devout in his church endeavor, and he takes sufficient time from his work to act as Superintendent of one of our largest Sunday Schools.

George changed the company name to Liberty Glass in 1918, when Liberty bonds were being sold; he also felt the name seemed quite appropriate for glass products. From all accounts he was a patriotic man who showed his love for his country by naming his company Liberty.

George Sr., who started in the glass industry as one of the youngest in the business, served as President of Liberty Glass up until six months before his death, when he retired due to health problems. He was succeeded by his son, George Jr, but retained the chairmanship of the board of directors until his death in 1939.

George Sr.'s obituary stated that while living in Sapulpa, before moving to Tulsa in 1927, he was active in the First Methodist Church, and his name is inscribed on the cornerstone as a member of the building committee. He was also a 32nd-degree Mason and was active in the Rotary Club, Chamber of Commerce and other civic groups.

In addition, George Sr. was known for his interest in American Shorthorn Cattle and was active in the American Shorthorn Breeder's Association.

Funeral services were held at the family home in Tulsa for George Sr., who was 66 years old at the time he died. George's wife, Jennie, had preceded her husband in death 10 years earlier. Thanks to a foundation George and Jennie established, their contributions and their names live on today.

SAPULPA DAILY HERALD

SAPULPA, OKLAHOMA TUESDAY, JUNE 18, 1957

THIS HUGE mass of broken concrete will soon be Home Plate in the Peewee baseball field to be built in the new Liberty Park in the northeast section of the city. Pictured here (pointing) are Dale Edan, member of the city planning commission, George Collins, Jr., Liberty Glass president, center, and Add Ellyson, city manager. The group was inspecting the site of the new park. (Photo by Jack Daudican.)

Collins Foundation To Give Sapulpa New Park

Sapulpa Daily Herald
June 18, 1957

The George and Jennie Collins Foundation announced that they would build a new park on the northeast 20 acres of the old city airport. They planned on building a peewee baseball field, picnic tables, outdoor fireplaces, a shelter house and other amenities. It would be called Liberty Park. This park now houses Liberty School, a baseball field, a new million-dollar aquatic center, a splash pad, tennis courts, volleyball court, a shelter and other playground equipment.

Frank Collins

Manager/Vice President of the Board
1918-1963

Frank Collins was the half-brother of George F. Collins Sr., and his vital partner in the glass business. Frank was the manager of Liberty Glass until his retirement in 1963. Uncle Frank, as he was known, served on the Liberty Board as Vice President, and also was employed as a consultant after his retirement. He worked with both his brother George Sr. and his nephew George Jr. for over fifty years. Both men relied heavily on Frank's expertise in the plant, but especially George Jr.

After his retirement Frank and his wife traveled extensively, visiting over 150 countries. He recorded these trips with a camera as photography was his favorite hobby.

Frank died in 1977 at age 91. Fittingly the casket bearers at his funeral were all employees from the Liberty Glass Plant.

Chapter Three

I Am Glass

Liberty Glass Company specializes in the manufacturing of *quality* glass containers for milk and beverage bottles.

George F. Collins Jr., heir to Liberty Glass after his father George Sr. died, commissioned a multi-media marketing campaign for Liberty Glass in the early 1960s. The approach was very sophisticated for a glass company in those days, but George was a visionary and wanted to let people know that Liberty was going places.

The final result was a descriptive, professional brochure coupled with a well-produced 16 - millimeter Color Sound Movie. Both told the Liberty Glass Story, and both included a beautifully written tribute to glass titled "I am Glass" by George J. Overmyer. Each also told a brief history of Liberty, along with a detailed description and flow-chart on how a Liberty Glass Bottle was made.

To this day, the multi-media presentation remains the most detailed look inside the Liberty Glass Plant ever produced.

FLOW CHART OF GLASS MANUFACTURING PROCESS...

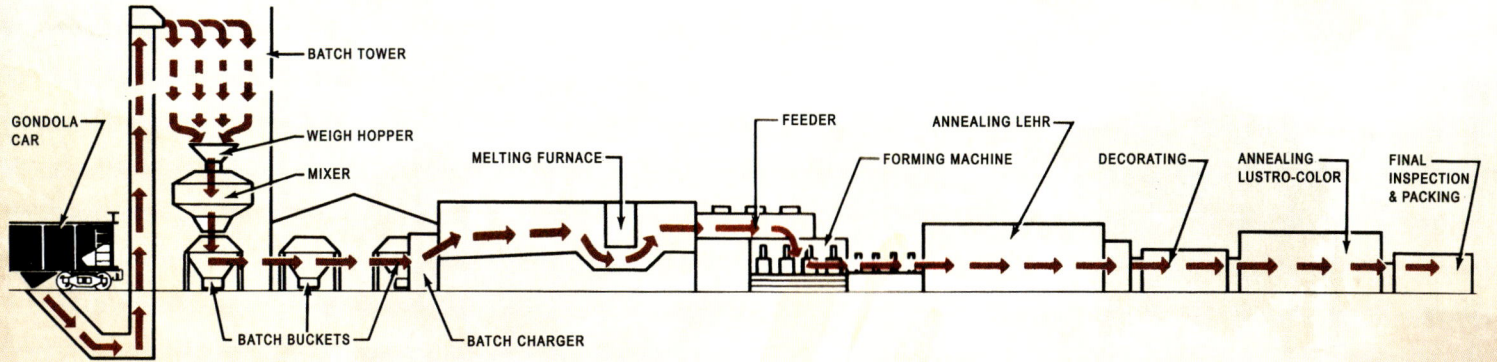

George F. Collins, Sr.,
Founder

George F. Collins, Jr.,
President

From a mere idea conceived in the mind of one of the industrial pioneers of the Southwest over 50 years ago, Liberty Glass Company today is an important factor in the glass container industry, having supplied returnable glass milk and beverage bottles over a territory extending from Alaska in the Artic to the Tropical Isles of the Caribbean and covering most of the United States.

Although Liberty was a war baby of World War I, Liberty was actually established in 1912 by the late George F. Collins Sr. under the name of the predecessor, Premium Glass Co., whose actual plant operations began in 1913. At one time Sapulpa was the home of four glass companies–Premium, Schramm, Sunflower and Bartlett-Collins.

After Premium was established, Mr. Collins formed a partnership with H.U. Bartlett and established the Bartlett-Collins Glass Company in 1915. The partnership was dissolved in 1918, and on August 5th of that year, Collins organized the Liberty Glass Company which took over the Premium plant and started to manufacture milk bottles and other glass containers. The Bartlett-Collins Company is still in operation and an important factor in the manufacture of glassware.

Mr. Collins was desirous of combining the raw materials, natural fuels and available native labor to transform Oklahoma's natural resources into finished products. They would supply an important market and contribute to the industrial development, wealth and prosperity of the area. Thus, in 1923, Liberty's founder organized the George F. Collins and Co., and established a glass container plant at Poteau, Oklahoma. Later, Collins dissolved the Collins Co. to consolidate the two plants under one operation and management at Sapulpa.

The Manufacturing Plant - Sapulpa

General Offices - Collins Building Sapulpa

From that time on, the Liberty Glass Company has enjoyed a consistent growth, specializing in the manufacture of milk and beverage bottles to better serve those two important industries.

Plant facilities have been increased and improved through the years. Factory force, sales department and jobbing connections have been expanded to provide its growing list of customers with better service and the newest in styles and finishes.

Today, Liberty is one of the nation's most progressive manufacturers of milk and beverage bottles.

Liberty is appreciative of the privilege of serving those customers whose patronage has made its own success and progress possible. The completion of major plant facilities adds substantially to the company's output and enables Liberty to better care for the requirements of its customers.

(Above) Reception lobby of the plant office typifies a light, pleasant place to work.

(Below) Exterior view of the plant office building shows the famed LG tower (raw materials storage and batch mixing) in the background. Plant office building is on North Mission Street in Sapulpa.

I Am Glass - The Liberty Story

I Am Glass

I am created of the admixture of Earth's minerals, formed by the alchemy of time

I am born transformed in the blasting heat of fiery furnace

In molten mass I am tediously fashioned by the hand of cunning Artisan - or fed into maw of intricate machine

I assume ten thousand hues of all the spectrum - either transparent, translucent or opaque - upon my maker's will

I can masquerade as ruby - emerald - topaz - moonstone, and all the other priceless jewels of man

But frivolous baubles are not my aspiration - I serve ten million purposes in as many different places, forms and ways

My duties are unnumbered - infinite; pay heed to my utility:

I admit the Heavenly light to hovel, palace or cathedral, and yet repel cold winter's howling breath

I faithfully project the light that warns great ships from shoal and concentrate the beams that guide swift vehicle through storm and gloom of night to bring the wayfarer safe home

I visibly contain my master's food - his drink - and his countless other of his commodities; protecting them in transport and in the mart and home

I form the shell of growing bulb and tube to diffuse his artificial light - and to disseminate his advertising

I am the walls of his abode, his office and his factory - and objects of utility and art in each of these

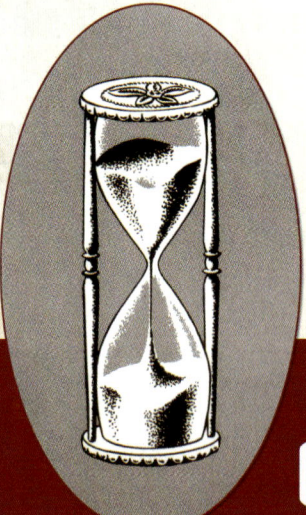

OLD AS THE SANDS OF TIME *Modern*

I reflect his image - and mark the effects of time upon his person - sometimes I flatter but more often am critically severe

I correct his impaired sight and thus bestow enjoyment of the printed word - and all of Nature's beauties roundabout

I magnify his minute, unseen enemies and thereby do I promote his health and happiness

I form the gossamer thread from which is fashioned fine raiment - yet too the insulation of this dwelling

I reveal to him the mysteries of his Universe - carrying his vision to the illimitable reaches of the outer stars

Through me he learned to chart the Firmament - to plat the orbits of the Planets and predict the courses of the Comets and Eclipses

This knowledge I unfold is but the pledge of vaster knowledge as - step by step - I lead him to unexplored, immeasurable spaces

For I am older than the Pyramids yet newer than tomorrow's unborn dawn - withal the marks of time affect me not - for I am ageless and retain my lustrous beauty permanently

Some of my tasks I have recounted - but this is only the beginning; for those who make me and adapt me to their uses, are men of vision - and together, as time unfolds, we will go far

And so - in modesty I proclaim - I am Man's invaluable and versatile servant - I AM GLASS

Copyright by George J. Overmyer

AS THE FACE OF TOMORROW

HOW A *Liberty Glass* BOTTLE IS MADE...

THE BATCH AND MELTING

(Left)
Materials are discharged from weight hopper into a tilting mixer, mixing approximately three tons of batch materials at one time.

(Below)
The weighing machine, through the use of vibrating feeders, can measure hundreds of pounds of ingredients that comprise the batch, down to the weight of an eyelash.

(Left)
Rugged yet sensitive. This aptly describes the automatic scales that tell when the batch has the proper amount of each ingredient down to the last ounce.

THE FURNACE

(Top)
The batch melting furnace in the background is fed its glass-making raw materials from the batch hoppers in the foreground.

(Top Left)
Track-tractor operator picks up the batch hopper after it is filled. Next step – it goes to the furnace batch charger.

(Bottom Left)
The Hartford-Empire furnace batch charger automatically feeds the furnace with batch on a continuous and controlled basis. The batch is made up principally of silica sand, soda ash, and limestone.

(Bottom Right)
These four Joy compressors in the huge plant provide the compressed air for blowing glass containers and cooling glass and equipment in the plant forming department. The glassblower's blowpipe is gone from the scene.

23

I Am Glass - The Liberty Story

THE MOULD

Automatically form-cutting the cavity of a blow mould on a duplicating lathe.

(Left) Craftsman engraving a beverage bottle blow mould made of special fine-grained iron.

Lacing design decoration is put on a milk bottle according to customer's order.

Machining the face joint of a blow mould.

Intricate decorations on beverage blow moulds express individuality and high quality of craftsmanship. Each mould must match a master mould exactly.

I Am Glass - The Liberty Story

FORMING

Dual forming of beverage bottles.

(Below)
Accurately timed gentle fingers of take-out arm lift this milk bottle from the blow mould to the conveyor.

Liberty FLAME-POLISH* dairy containers coming out of the blow moulds.

Fire-finished beverage bottles being lifted to the conveyor.

*A Liberty Trade-Mark

I Am Glass - The Liberty Story

ANNEALING, SELECTING & PACKING

(Top) Uniform placement of bottles in annealing lehr (oven) by a Liberty designed loader.

(Middle) Annealed bottles reach the cool end of the annealing lehr.

(Right) Protective surface coating of glass containers at the packing end of the annealing lehr.

Panoramic view of COMANCHE* Model 120 decorating machine with auxiliary equipment.

*COMANCHE equipment supplied by Applied Color Equipment Company, a Liberty Glass Company subsidiary.

DECORATING

(Middle Left) Artists prepare layouts for designs or decorations to be used with LUSTRO-COLOR* ceramic enamels. (*A LIBERTY TRADEMARK)

(Middle Right) Our COMANCHE MODEL 120 automatic decorating machine applying multicolor designs.

(Bottom Left) The decorating lehr heats the LUSTRO-COLOR decorations to the right temperature so they become part of the glass for increased trippage.

I Am Glass - The Liberty Story

The polariscope grades the annealing properties of glass by showing strains in characteristic colors.

QUALITY CONTROL LABORATORY

(Right) View of capacity testing machine.

(Bottom) View of quality control laboratory. The machine, right foreground, is a hydrostatic internal-pressure tester for beverage bottles.

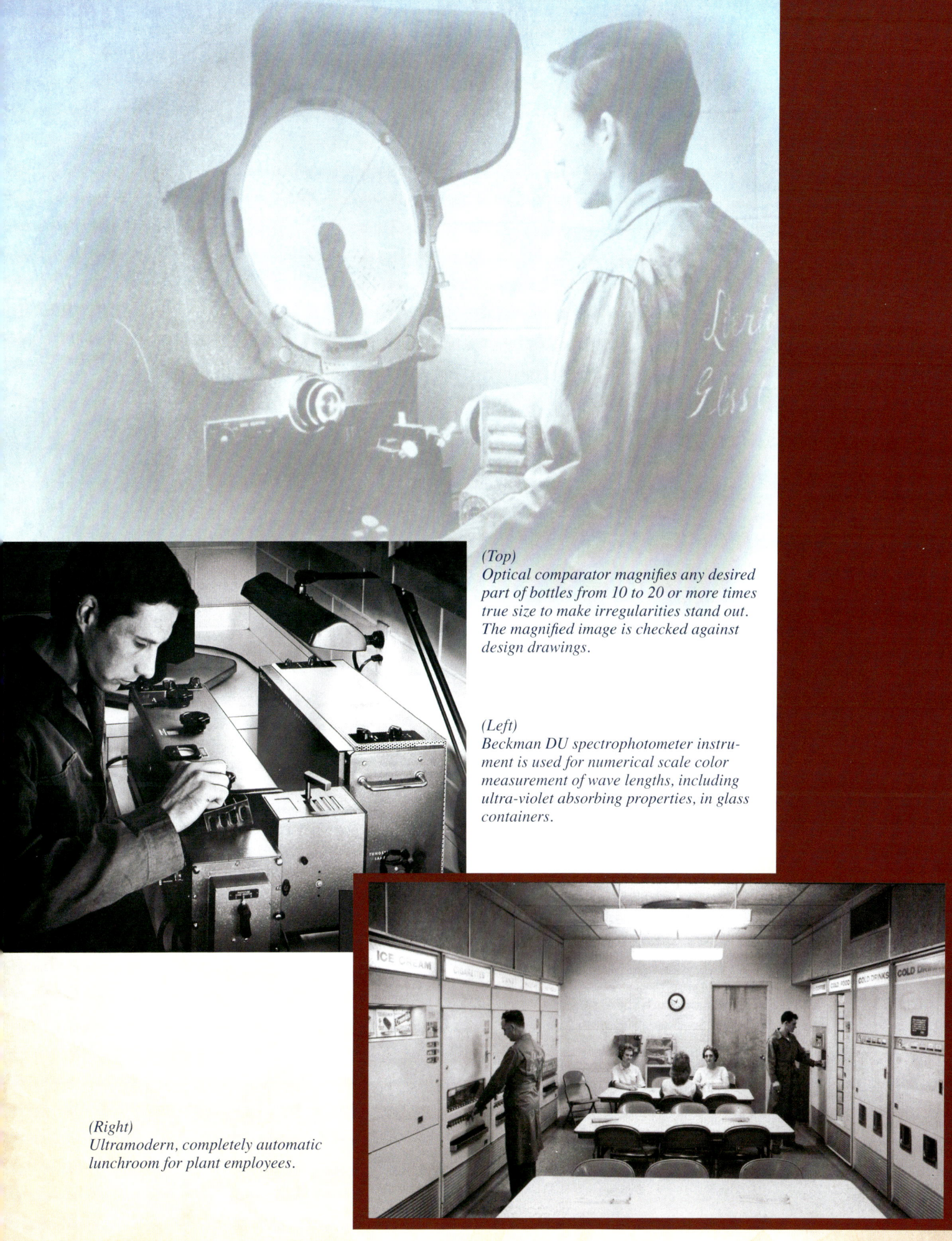

(Top)
Optical comparator magnifies any desired part of bottles from 10 to 20 or more times true size to make irregularities stand out. The magnified image is checked against design drawings.

(Left)
Beckman DU spectrophotometer instrument is used for numerical scale color measurement of wave lengths, including ultra-violet absorbing properties, in glass containers.

(Right)
Ultramodern, completely automatic lunchroom for plant employees.

STORING & SHIPPING

Symmetry in glass. A quick glance reminds one of an ultramodern office building. A closer look shows neatly stacked trays of beverage bottles.

(Left) Lift-truck operator stacks a pallet of beverage bottle trays in the warehouse.

(Below) Gallon milk bottles are stacked in the warehouse on pallets.

(Above) View of increased warehouse built in recent years as part of continuing expansion program.

THATS THE END OF OUR STORY...
BUT FOR A *Liberty* BOTTLE, IT'S ONLY THE BEGINNING.

Loading Liberty bottles onto truck for shipment to customers throughout the country.

DISTRIBUTION

Another Liberty Service

THE GLASSER
Liberty's Weather Bulletin
460 SOUTH BROADWAY
DENVER 9, COLORADO

The Glasser published monthly by Liberty Glass Company.

Monthly Forecast

Legend: ▥ COOL ▆ WARM ■ PRECIP. ☐ SEASONALLY NORMAL WEATHER

AREA I. Oklahoma and Kansas

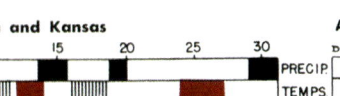

A cold and wet month is indicated. Most days will be in the 60s and 70s although during the warm spells temperatures will rise into the 80s. Some of the colder mornings will develop around the 10th and 16th. Relatively wet weather is in prospect during the first 7 days of the month. Around the 15th and 19th more showers will develop. A spell of generally drier weather will prevail between the 20th and 28th of the month which will be relatively favorable for sales of bottled beverages. More stormy weather will move in by the 29th.

AREA II. Texas

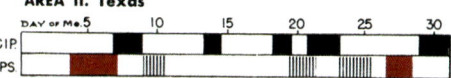

Temperatures will range from below normal in the Panhandle region to near normal in the southern sections of the State. The first 5 to 6 days will be generally mild although some showers will affect the northern parts of the State early in the month. The more significant precipitation will develop by the 8th. Other periods of unfavorable weather are due near the 14th, between the 19th and 23rd and on several days near the end of October. The interval starting about the 19th will be predominantly cool and wet with the better sales weather developing again by the 26th.

AREA III. Arkansas and Missouri

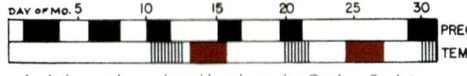

Look for weather to be cold and wet this October. Conditions are not especially favorable for sales of bottled beverages. Storms will develop frequently during the month especially during the first 20 days. Better conditions will set up during the last third of October although by the 30th it will be stormy and cold again.

AREA IV. Colorado and New Mexico

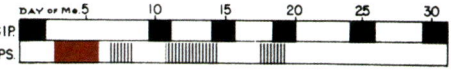

A rather cold and stormy October is forecast for this region. The month will start off stormy with warmer conditions developing by the 3rd or 4th. Relatively cool conditions will affect the region by the 7th with a more important cold outbreak coming during the interval between the 10th and 15th. Weather systems from the west will be moving through with regularity. From the standpoint of bottled beverages the best weather conditions will develop around the 4th with a fair interval also on several days between the 20th and 30th.

AREA V. Louisiana, Mississippi and Western Tennessee

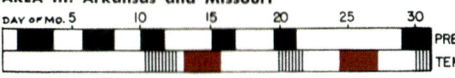

[There] will be several penetrations of cold air into the region [the] month will be an unusually cool one. Look for some of [the] nights to develop between the 10th and 22nd of the [month]s also will develop frequently. Showers will be [occurring] the first 10 days, again on several days around [the] 8th.

AREA VI. Alabama, Georgia, Florida, Eastern Tennessee and Carolinas

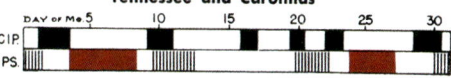

The outlook is for cool and wet weather this October. Storms are expected to move through the region fairly frequently with some of the better sales weather developing around the 5th and 25th of October. The cooler mornings are due near the 1st, 11th, and 21st. During these periods relatively low temperature readings can be expected in the northern sections of Alabama, Georgia and in Tennessee and the Carolinas with local frost likely.

AREA VII. Arizona, California, Nevada and Utah

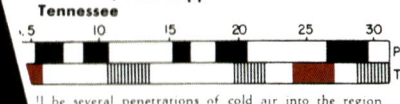

[The fir]st half of the month will be generally favorable for sale[s of] bottled beverages. Relatively mild and dry conditions will [preva]il whereas by the second half of October stormy and cool[er we]ather will predominate. Weather will be especially wet alon[g th]e California Coast although most of this region will experi[enc]e cloudy and unsettled weather between the 17th and 27th. Ove[ral]l moisture will be above normal with temperatures aver[ag]in[g] near to below normal.

AREA VIII. Minnesota, Wisconsin, Iowa, Illinois, Michigan, Indiana and Kentucky

Here too below normal temperatures are in prospect. Arctic air will make frequent intrusions into this region resulting in temperatures much below normal. Storms also will develop frequently resulting in wet and cloudy weather during most of the month. Some improvement is expected late in the month when a spell of warm and dry weather is indicated.

AREA IX. Montana, Wyoming, Dakotas and Nebraska

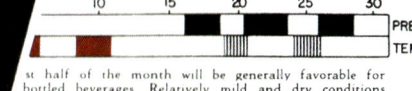

Below normal temperatures are expected. Conditions will be mild early in October but turning colder near the 7th, 17th and 28th. Storms will develop quite frequently especially the first 15 days resulting in a rather dismal outlook from the standpoint of sales. A rather general storm will develop around the 10th to 14th. After mid-month precipitation will develop less frequently but still predominantly cool.

AREA X. Washington, Oregon and Idaho

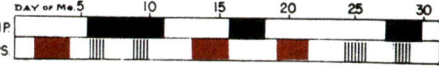

Look for scattered showers to occur early in the month; otherwise the first 5 days will be predominantly fair and mild. Starting about the 6th several days of cloudy and stormy weather are expected. Conditions will improve by the 12th with warming temperatures by the 14th. Look for more rain in the area near the 17th warm again by the 20th with showers occurring intermittently between the 22nd and the 24th. Some of the colder weather will develop near the 25th and 27th with more precipitation overspreading the region during the last 2 or 3 days of October.

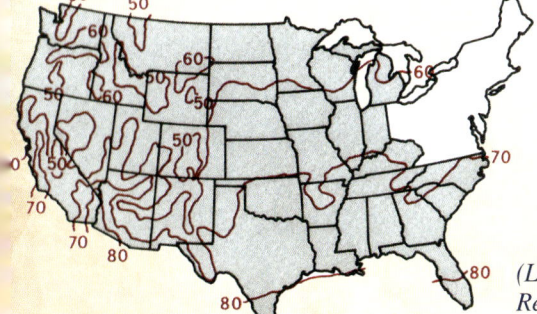

(Left) Shaded portion shows our distribution territory. Red lines indicate average normal monthly temperatures.

Copyright, Irving P. Kirk

I Am Glass - The Liberty Story

Chapter Four

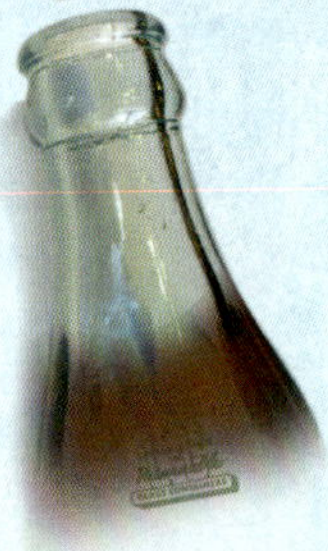

The First Family of Liberty Glass
Part 2

The Generations Change... but the Family Endures...

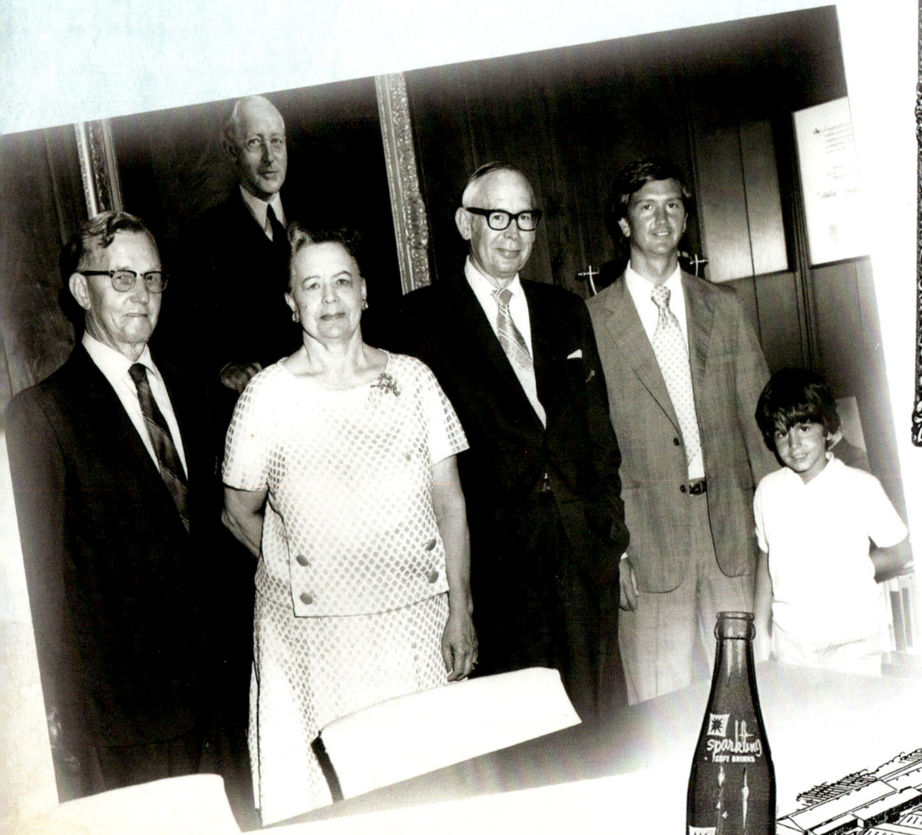

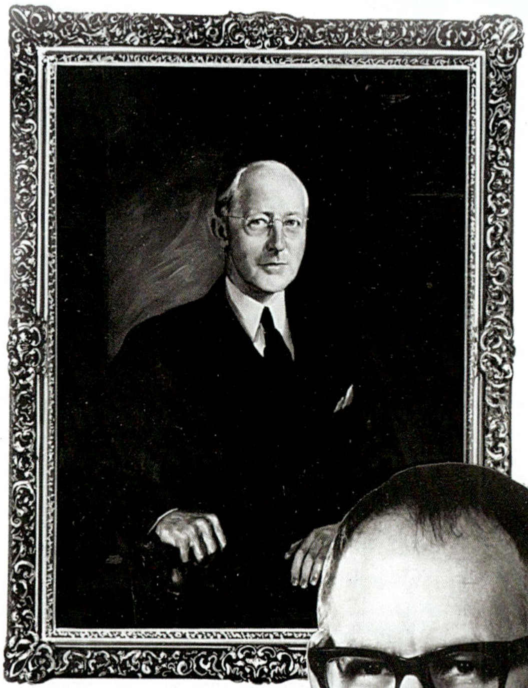

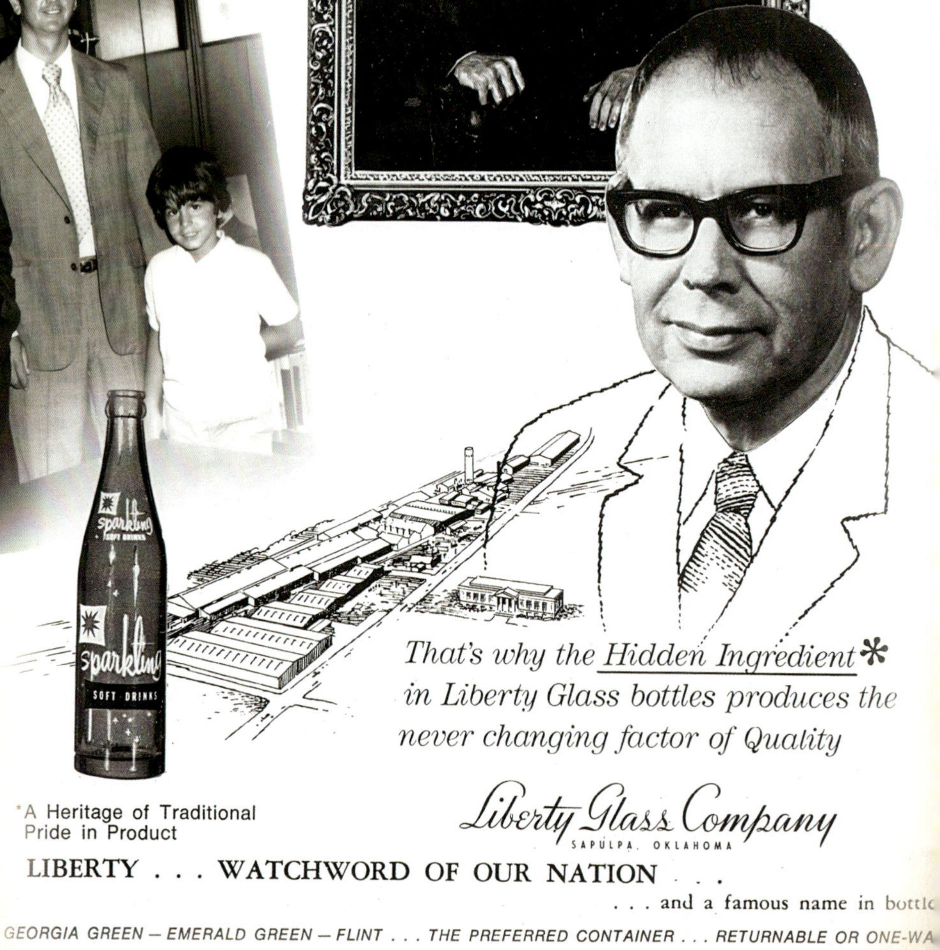
sparkling
SOFT DRINKS
That's why the Hidden Ingredient*
in Liberty Glass bottles produces the
never changing factor of Quality
*A Heritage of Traditional
Pride in Product
Liberty Glass Company
SAPULPA, OKLAHOMA
LIBERTY . . . WATCHWORD OF OUR NATION . . .
. . . and a famous name in bottle
GEORGIA GREEN — EMERALD GREEN — FLINT . . . THE PREFERRED CONTAINER . . . RETURNABLE OR ONE-WA

George F. Collins, Jr.

Chief Executive Officer
1939-1980

After the death of his father in 1939, George F. Collins Jr. inherited Liberty Glass at a very early age. He was in his 20s when he took over the company, which at the time was loaded with debt. George would go on to lead the company for over four decades, but his later years were impacted by very poor health.

Even though George had no formal degree, his youngest son Roger said his dad never stopped studying and learning, always trying to stay on the leading edge of the glass industry.

Roger Collins Son of George Collins Jr. Management 1977-1981	*"From a business standpoint, he managed by looking at what his competitors were doing and studying his competitors and reading reports page by page and really trying to emulate what they were doing. He also talked to friends in the industry and vendors about what his competitors were doing. He tried to stay on the leading edge by doing those things."*
Beverley Collins Ward Daughter of George Collins Jr.	*"My father was such the businessman…always working even on Saturdays."*
Jim Bolin Plant Manager/President 1977-1994	*"His style was lead by committee with Frank Collins [George Jr.'s uncle] in charge."*

Kitty Hunt, the longtime secretary to George Jr., remembers him as a good leader, but often intimidating to those who worked for him. She says it was her job as his secretary to serve as a "gatekeeper" and only those he wanted to see or talk to could get through the gate.

Kitty Hunt
Secretary to George Collins Jr.
1967-1980

"I was a liaison between Mr. Collins and everybody else in the world."

"I was on call 24 hours a day. That I did not know before I started."

Johnny L. Brison
Plant Maintenance Supervisor
1959-1994

"I didn't know a lot about George or how he was. I originally thought George Collins was the type of guy that didn't really like the people that worked out there, but he really did! When they made that movie [I Am Glass], he took all the "I"s out of that opening speech. If you read that, there are no "I"s. He said, 'I can't do anything, but WE can conquer the world'. And I thought boy that was the nicest thing I ever heard. It meant a lot to me. He was a people's guy in a lot of ways. I thought he was a pretty good guy, but he sure didn't believe in giving money away." (laugh)

No doubt this statement by George Jr. meant a lot to Liberty's people at the time. Those who worked closely with him say he was very reserved at the office, but in contrast he is also remembered as a man who liked to have fun. Reports from some of those who attended sales conventions with him noted George was much more relaxed out of the office and loved to kick up his heels and dance at the convention parties. These reports often made their way back to the gossip groups at Liberty, who from all indication found this rather amusing since George was always so reserved at the office.

David Beyer
Accounting Department
Chief Financial Officer
1972-1994

"He was a different person at work than he was away from work. I did travel with him some."

"When he was here at the office he thought he had to put on a certain persona. But when he was away from work and we were at a meeting he was the life of the party, told jokes, everybody loved him. He had story after story after story."

Roger Collins
Son of George Collins Jr.
Management
1977-1981

"He loved to play games. He played a lot of bridge and he played a lot of backgammon. I have a lot of fond memories of him playing backgammon and chess."

Susie Collins
Wife of Fulton Collins

"He loved to travel…George traveled the world."

"He loved to play practical jokes."

Beverley Collins Ward
Daughter of
George Collins Jr.

"He and my mom would have huge parties at our wonderful home on 41st and Lewis."

The First Family of Liberty Glass - Part 2

Kitty Hunt
Secretary to George Collins Jr.
1967-1980

"He loved the telephone. He had some golf clubs he carried everywhere but he never played. He would play cards, he played bridge."

George also liked ping pong. The game became a big part of his daily routine, as he and three others held spirited matches during lunch at the Collins building. However, there was one unwritten Golden Rule during the games that no one dared to break.

David Beyer
Accounting Department
Chief Financial Officer
1972-1994

"We played partners. Four of us played and 95% of the time I was always George Collins' partner. It was Windy Davis, purchasing agent and the plant manager and we would play three games. The first two we always split, but the third game we always won because George was supposed to win."

"Windy and whoever Windy played with would let us split the first two and then we would always win the third. It was always a very competitive game, but we always knew we were going to win the third game so George could win the match. It was a tradition. George knew what was happening."

"My career at the Liberty Glass Company was helped as much by what I knew about ping pong as what I knew about finance. Ping pong may have helped me more."

George's first wife was Beverly Lorton, with whom he had three children, George III, called Fulton, Beverley and a second son, Roger.

Beverly Lorton was the widow of Robert Lorton Sr., a member of the Tulsa World publishing dynasty. The couple had one son, Robert Lorton Jr., known as Bobby Lorton. However, Bobby Lorton became Bobby Collins when his mother married George Jr. His own father had died when the boy was very young and Beverly wanted her son to carry the Collins name. Perhaps she felt this would help him better adjust to being part of a new family.

After growing up a Collins, however, Bobby returned to his original name of Robert Lorton Jr. He was last in the line of Lortons, and he wanted his father's name to continue into future generations.

Robert Lorton Jr. would go on to become the longtime CEO of the Tulsa World. One of the city's most respected leaders, Bob and his son Bobby continued to run the newspaper until it sold in early 2013.

Today, Bob Lorton recalls one of his first summer jobs in the plant at Liberty Glass.

Robert Lorton Jr.
Stepson of George Collins Jr.
Plant Worker
1953-1954

"As I recall, it was a summer when we had a week to ten days with temperatures over 100 degrees. I worked in the plant where the furnaces are over 2,000 degrees (I think). I had a tank tender job and would wear an overcoat and gloves and hat to get close to the viewing port on the glass tank. I survived on Dr. Pepper and salt tablets. Thank goodness I didn't do this very long. Sometimes I would get so dirty I took my clothes off before going into our house. Mother's rules!"

George Collins Jr. and Beverly divorced when the children were still young and she moved the two youngest, Beverley and Roger, back to the East Coast where she was raised. Fulton was already in the east attending preparatory school.

George, now a very eligible bachelor, later married a beautiful Tulsa socialite, Mimi Fair. Many agree his personal life was often complicated, much like the man himself.

Jackie Rule Robertson
Accounting Department
1942-1943

"I remember George got married while I was there and came around and asked everybody what they wanted, cigars or candy. Naturally I didn't say I wanted cigars, but anyway he went around the whole office to see what we wanted."

Those who knew the couple say Mimi shared George's passion for bridge and other card games. They often entertained at their beautiful Tulsa mansion, which still sits majestically on the corner of 41st and Lewis.

Doris Yocham, whose husband was in the sales department for 28 years, remembers visiting George and Mimi at the Collins home.

Doris Yocham
Wife of Dick Yocham in Sales Department
1956-1984

"I do not believe he could have been any nicer, he was a very gracious host."

"We had a very good relationship with him."

Today Roger Collins recalls that his dad continued to play a big part in his life, and visited the family often after they moved to the East Coast with their mother. As he reminisced, Roger also remembered a number of lessons he learned from his dad, but perhaps none greater than this.

Roger Collins
Son of George Collins Jr.
Management
1977-1981

"One is to listen to people around you. He did that."

"He liked to involve others in his decision making. He had quarterly board meetings when all the senior management would come in and he would listen to them. That was his management style."

Another family member, Fulton Collins' wife Susie, says she got along famously with her father-in-law. Because of her work as a teacher, she remembers the special bond she shared with George Jr.

Susie Collins
Wife of Fulton Collins

"He was passionate about education. I think he attended seven colleges, but never graduated from any of them."

George Collins Jr. died from emphysema in 1980. He was ill for a number of years before his death and as a result, experienced some difficulties running the company.

However, David Beyer remembers one particular day when George had no problem running anything and clearly showed great strength in spite of his failing health.

David Beyer
Accounting Department
Chief Financial Officer
1972-1994

"The worst day was when I was fired. Jim Bolin, the plant manager and I were fired together. We had discounted pricing to Oklahoma City Coke and Mr. Collins was in the office less and less due to his failing health. We didn't check with him….he was at home. We had a meeting over the phone. He went down the list. He fired Jim Bolin and he fired David Beyer. And then he fired that Collins kid [Roger]. We didn't know what to do. So Jim said we should just go back to work. The next day we went back to work and nobody ever said a word about it."

Tribute to the memory of
GEORGE FULTON COLLINS, JR.
1916-1980
PRESIDENT AND CHAIRMAN OF THE BOARD
Liberty Glass Company
SAPULPA, OKLAHOMA

Those who were close to George Collins Jr. say he put up a brave front right up to the end, even though he knew his days were numbered. After his death he was eulogized as a man with many special qualities, as illustrated in this Glasser Magazine tribute written by Floyd Gates.

Tribute by Floyd Gates

Head Sculpture Jay O'Melia

Portrait from Painting by E. Raymond Kinstler

GEORGE F. COLLINS, JR.

This is a tribute to his unstinting service and dedication for 42 years as guiding hand in both spirit and policy in his position as President and Chairman of the Board of Liberty Glass Company. He was a zealous and untiring worker in civic and philanthropic causes and for foundations bearing his name especially in the fields of education and medical research.

He was a lover and collector of art and a devotee of sports, loving tennis with a passion attested to by the gift of beautiful lighted courts to the city of Sapulpa.

Wielding a firm and positive hand in all his business dealings, he was held in high regard throughout the industry for his integrity and sense of fair play.

Loyalty to friends and devotion to family were hallmarks of his character, while pride in the people and workers in his company fueled his amazing drive.

He was possessed with an almost worshipful devotion to the memory of his father, whose death when George was only twenty-three years of age saddled him with responsibilities which would have staggered a man of twice his age and experience.

He viewed his position as a challenge to live up to his father's expectations of him as being worthy to bear the Collins name.

George F. Collins, Jr. would have liked nothing better said of him than that he was really and truly his father's son.

"My students are benifited through facilities and the knowledge that someone cares about them and their university."
Marion K. Roberts, Director of bands, Baker University

"We have lost a good friend and one of the kindest, and most generous men I have ever known."
William L. Hannah
Glass Container Group

"I was greatly impressed with his competence and his sense of the needs of humanity"
Bob Kohle Baker University
Dean of the college

"The George F. Collins Stadium has made other schools envious of our fine facility."
Board of Education,
Sapulpa Public Schools
Larry Higgs, President

Loreine Collins Dietrich

Senior Vice President and Director
1943-1983

When George Collins Jr. served as President of Liberty, it was his older sister Loreine, who played the role of First Lady. The siblings were very close and affectionately referred to each other as "brother" and "sister" even into adulthood.

Kitty Hunt
Secretary to George Collins Jr.
1967-1980

"He got to where he'd lean on his sister… Mrs. Dietrich wanted him to lean on her."

Mrs. Dietrich served as Senior Vice President and Director of the company for more than 40 years. During that time one of her duties was to serve as Editor of the Glasser Newsletter. This publication was sent out periodically by the company to customers, employees and others who had a connection or interest in the glass business.

Interestingly, the Glasser featured weather updates, as Liberty customers were mostly soft drink bottlers and sales were always affected by the weather.

John Conway
Technical Director Assistant/Sales/
Assistant Director of Marketing
1968-1979

Red Ball Trucking VP of Operations/
Director of Marketing
1981-1990

"The Glasser's big importance was that it accurately forecast the weather. This allowed our beverage customers the ability to plan their own promotions based on accurate forecasts, which are extremely important for beverage customers. In addition to attracting our customers to work together with us, it also helped them forecast more accurately their own glass needs and ultimately help us schedule and run more efficiently."

The newsletter also contained items of interest about Liberty, such as its latest products and improvements, or interesting stories about the company and its employees, all of which helped bring the company closer to its customers.

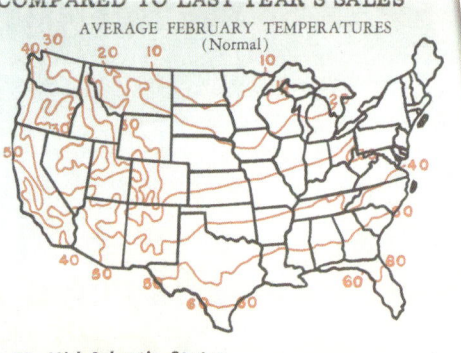

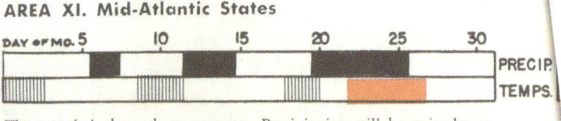

From Your Glasser Editor...

Nearing New Year's Eve, 1982 — We bring you Greetings for the New Year of 1983 and also a farewell copy of our "Glasser". This medium has been a line of communication from Liberty Glass Company to our customers for over thirty years. We are proud of our "Freedom Foundation" Award for patriotic content during the Bi-centennial years and of the artwork by our friend and artist, Floyd Gates, who created the recent series "Southwestern Country Life-at Turn of the Century". We have enjoyed our long relationship with Irving P. Krick who has supplied our weather bulletins since 1952.

It has been a pleasure to serve as editor of our "Glasser". This house organ, initiated by my brother, the late George Fulton Collins, Jr., has served to introduce new personnel and new products to you. Now, with changing times, we are discontinuing our "Glasser"... with hopes that we can find new and better ways to keep in touch with all our "Glasser" friends.

With warmest wishes to you all,

Loreine C. Dietrich, editor
Senior Vice President
Liberty Glass Company

Liberty Glass Company
SAPULPA, OKLAHOMA 74066

Mrs. Dietrich had various other responsibilities and for those who remember working with her, most say she was a force to be reckoned with at Liberty. Sales Department Receptionist Linda Campbell remembers Mrs. Dietrich invoked some very strict guidelines when it came to office dress and behavior.

Linda Campbell
Sales Department
Receptionist

"One day one of the girls had on a white blouse with a black bra and she made her go home."

There were others who seemed to be intimidated by Mrs. Dietrich's steely nature. Even the forceful Sales Manager, Wills Young, and Plant Manager, Jim Bolin remember facing the wrath of Loreine Collins Dietrich.

Wills Young
Sales Department
Vice President
1980-1994

"I asked Roger one day...what does she do, who is that? She was unhappy about something and I don't know what it was."

"She kept giving me a hard time."

Jim Bolin
Plant Manager/President
1977-1994

"It's 110 outside, it's even hotter in the plant and the plant is dilapidated and you're fightin' to make money and that happened to be that August when we're starting to turn a curve. Mrs. Dietrich called me up and wants me to pull weeds outside the plant and I said to her that was not my priority and she said the place has got to look good."

"And then she started on flower beds around behind the building."

"I fixed the flower beds. (laugh) I called Johnny Brison in plant maintenance and had him take care of it."

Johnny L. Brison
Plant Maintenance
1953-1994

"I concreted them in because he told me to. I said they're gonna' fire us."

Perhaps at the time there were some who just weren't used to strong women. After all this was right at the beginning of the women's movement and maybe Mrs. Dietrich was just a little ahead of her time.

A number of employees at Liberty say they remember that Mrs. Dietrich made a special effort to help the women at the company succeed. This may have been her way of addressing the gender gap that was evident in almost all industries of the time.

Vickie Varnell Beyer
Accounting Department
1974-1976
1983-1990

"She was a lot of fun, always very kind to me. At one point after I had taken care of some things for her library, she came in and said, 'Young lady you're accepted now'. I knew then she was very satisfied."

Linda Campbell
Sales Department
Receptionist

"She made us respectful of our job, of our gender, of where we were. She made us feel special."

Mrs. Dietrich's nephew Roger Collins says he also gives his aunt credit for many good things that took place at Liberty Glass.

Roger Collins
Son of George Collins Jr.
Management
1977-1981

"I think my aunt should take a lot of credit for being nice to the people and getting my dad to continually think about the people and what was going on."

"She was a character. Several of us didn't want her meddling in some things, but with time as a guide looking back I think she actually accomplished some good things."

"She never did have any kids and she went through several husbands. I'm not sure what the count was, but more than one. My dad kind of took her under his wing. She was an older sister to him. She was quite a bit older. He took her under his wing and created a position for her."

Russell Crosby Tulsa Sapulpa Union Railway Vice President/General Manager 1974-Present	*"I always remember on your birthday, when you got home there was a birthday card in the mailbox. I thought that was a neat gesture."*
Roger Collins Son of George Collins Jr. Management 1977-1981	*"She organized birthday get-togethers and thank you [parties], and she was in charge of making sure all employees got a birthday card when their birthday came around and that was no small task."* *"I think she really wanted everyone to feel like it was a family business and that they were part of the family and that they would be taken care of."*

Everyone agrees, education was one of Mrs. Dietrich's primary passions, and caring for those in need was one of her life-long goals. She worked tirelessly with the Day Center for the Homeless and was responsible for establishing a number of scholarship opportunities.

Alynne Giese Sales Department/Quality Control 1960-1988	*"She had a scholarship to a Bible study if anyone wanted to go with a professor from TU."*

Mrs. Dietrich also funded scholarships for college students in Oklahoma as well as Baker University in Kansas, her father's alma mater.

The First Family of Liberty Glass - Part 2

Proud of her heritage, Mrs. Dietrich was a member of the Daughters of the American Revolution. She also began the Oklahoma chapter of the Sons and Daughters of the Pilgrims and was the past national president of the U.S. Daughters of 1812 and a national board member of the Daughters of Colonial Wars.

Beverley Collins Ward
Daughter of George Collins Jr.

> "Aunt Loreine was very conscientious about the Daughters of the American Revolution. She enjoyed her membership and had many caring friends in her group. She cared about our family history and had a huge library in her home. When I was a little girl (8-10) she had me join a golf group, and I played tournaments in the neighboring towns as well as in Tulsa. She took great pride in me doing that."

Loreine Dietrich retired from Liberty in 1983, but seemingly never retired from life. She lived in Tulsa until her death in 1995 at age 91.

(Below) Poems written by Loreine Dietrich.

There's Always A Tommorrow

Look ahead
Leave today behind

There are only twenty-four hours
in each section of time

You know it
I know it

Look ahead
Leave today behind

But it has been such
a good day

I want it to go on forever
And stop - never.

Look ahead
Leave today behind

There is always a tomorrow.

At the Airport

The clitter and clutter
of movements to and fro
Halting, running
fast and slow.

The moving picture
remains the same
People of all color
dress and speech

Stop the camera
Wherever you are
Dallas, Dover, Denver, Dakar

With the spirit of quest
Curiosity is restless.

Hurry home, Leave it
Meet and part
At the airport listen for
the beat of the heart.

A Tear

I feel a tear on my cheek.
Why is it there?

I've been asleep
In a chair by the fire.

I talked to Brother
He was going away

I said, Write to me
Take care of yourself

Here, I'll give you
an envelope addressed to me

So we'll keep in touch.
I love you so much.

Then a tear hit my cheek
As I awoke from the dream

But it did seem that I had
talked to my Brother.

Was it a dream?

An oldie

Don't be afraid of being old
You'll never get to be old.
Here, take my hand
I'll show you the way.
But, wait, should I tell you
my way-
I declare it wouldn't be fair
To hear my story,
That's mine
And that's fine.
Just know that there is joy
and love and despair and
happiness beyond compare
and woes and problems
you can't overcome but you do.
That's the 'shew'.
So frolic along and be serious too.
Take another's hand, Be a friend
and you'll have one too.
the going is tough.
It gets rough.
But, see, you're still here.
So go along as best you can.
Be a friend and you'll have a friend.
That's what counts in the end.

DAR
Daughters of the
American Revolution

TRIBUTE TO MRS. IRA JONATHAN DIETRICH (Loreine Collins Dietrich)
19 July 1903 — 22 April 1995
Elected to Membership May 14, 1959   National No. 17146
PRESIDENT NATIONAL, NSUSD 1812
1970-1973

Loreine was born in Richmond, Texas, and lived her early life in Coffeyville, Kansas, from whence she moved with her [par]ents and brother to Sapulpa, Oklahoma, to establish what became the Liberty Glass Company. She was Senior Vice President and [on]e of the Directors for more than forty years, retiring in 1983. She was a graduate at Sapulpa High School and Kansas University. Her [br]other, affectionately called "Brother" by many friends, was reared mostly by Lo, since their parents died at a relatively early age. [T]hat brother was Mr. George F. Collins, Jr., who died in 1980.

Lo was a philanthropist. She worked with the Day Center for the Homeless helping that organization with needed funds and supplies. She was a Founding Trustee of the George and Jennie Collins Foundation, and the George F. Collins, Jr. Foundation. She founded several organizations at Baker University in Baldwin, Kansas, including the Ira J. Dietrich Scholarship Fund, the Excellence in Teaching Fund which provided money for educators, and the Isaac M. Landis Fund which provides Bibles to incoming freshmen. She was a member of the Oklahoma State and the Sapulpa Historical Societies, the Oklahoma Heritage Society, the Oklahoma Health and Welfare Association, the Tulsa Boys' Home Board, the first Secretary of the Frances E. Willard Home, and a Trustee of the Sapulpa Library. Also, she organized junior golf as a part of the Women's Oklahoma Golf Association, and enjoyed golf and tennis very much.

Lo was a member of the First United Methodist Church of Tulsa. She helped build the Methodist Mission in Cookson for the benefit of Cherokee Indians. She belonged to many of the patriotic-lineage societies and gave freely of her time, talent, resources and hospitality to promote the welfare and prosperity of those societies in which she so fervently believed, knowing that all are instru[ments] for the betterment of this country and its citizens. Included were the Oklahoma Branch of the National Society Sons and Daughters of the Pilgrims which she organized, the National Society of the United States Daughters of 1812 of which she was President National, and was a National Board and State Board Member of the National Society Daughters of Colonial Wars. She built a wing on her large home to house her important genealogical library noted far and wide as a vast and valuable library.

This generous lady loved the opera, musicals, theatre, was outgoing, friendly, humorous and always at hand when a friend was troubled. An example, I was hospitalized in Washington, D.C. for three days, having cataract surgery. Lo came from her home in Tulsa, managed to get a bed in my room, and watched over me 24 hours a day all those days. She endeared herself to the doctors, nurs[es] and aides. She was religious—quiet about it—but studious, serious, and a regular attendant at her church. Her death came a[fter a] valiant fight with cancer and a heart ailment. She was thoroughly knowledgeable of her condition and her short life expecta[n]cy; she died with courage, dignity and trust in God. I am a better person for having been friends with her for nearly [...] made business, funeral and other arrangements, even sending flowers to my sister and to me for our birthdays several days [before] death in the Dallas Hospital. She was composed, confident of her faith in God, and awaited the transition from this Life t[...] She had a zest for life and added energy to the world rather than draining energy from it. Yes, she lived with zest and a[...]

"Jimmy" her husband, preceded Lo in death, having died in 1976. She is survived by three nephews, one [...] and a half-sister. The recent bomb explosion in Oklahoma City which destroyed a large Federal office building, [...] ple and wounding many others, necessitated the raising of funds, millions-billions of dollars, and the Oklahoma C[...] Fund became the recipient of monetary gifts rather than floral tributes—further example of the family's ever gen[erous ...]

Loreine Dietrich was industrious, honest, tolerant, and last but not least—had the respect, confide[nce ...] colleagues. Having discovered that bourne from which no traveler returns, she is reunited with her precious [...] and we, though saddened, rejoice that we had the privilege of living in the presence of so noble, so just, so fine [...] intoned expression was never more fitting than to Loreine—Well Done, Thou Good and Faithful Servant.

May the immortal soul of Loreine Collins Dietrich enjoy forever the reward of blissful rest and peace.

Anne Carter Baldwin Holle
(Mrs. Charles George Holle)

U.S. Daughters of 1812 NEWS-LETTER

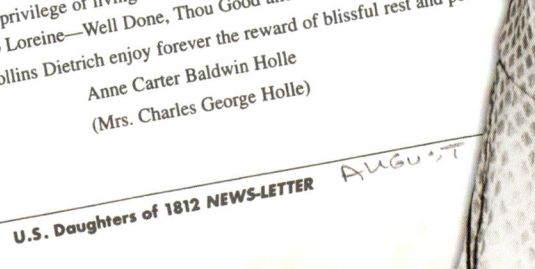

Roger Collins

Son of George Collins Jr.
Management
1977-1981

Unlike his father before him, Roger Collins had a very formal education and earned degrees at some of the best schools in higher education.

The youngest son of George Collins Jr., Roger received his undergraduate degree in electrical engineering from Princeton University and next earned an MBA from the prestigious Wharton School of Business.

Roger spent his early years in Tulsa, but his parents divorced when he was only five and the young boy moved to the East Coast with his mother. He didn't return to Oklahoma until after graduate school, and even though Roger didn't live with his father much of the time he was growing up, he said his dad visited him often.

Rogers's first experience at Liberty Glass came in the form of a summer job in 1976, between his first and second years at Wharton. After graduating in 1977, he returned to Liberty full-time even though that was not what he had planned to do. Initially, Roger hoped to stay on the East Coast and go into management consulting, but his dad convinced his son to return to Oklahoma and work for the family glass business. Unbeknownst to Roger, his father was seriously ill at the time and wanted his son by his side.

Roger Collins
Son of George Collins Jr.
Management
1977-1981

"He knew at the time he was dying, he knew he had emphysema. I didn't know this until after he died and I was going through his desk, but he knew as early as '74 or '75 that he was dying. The doctors had told him he wasn't going to live as long as he did."

Because of Roger's educational background, he says his dad first brought him into the company to oversee the IT Department. Almost everyone agrees, it was here Roger made one of his most significant contributions to Liberty.

David Block
IT Department Manager
1967-1994

"Roger Collins designed an absolute state-of-the-art computer center for Liberty Glass with raised floors. It was probably the best computer system in a 6-state region."

Roger said he eventually evolved into a self-described "Jack of all Trades" for Liberty. That's because he had to take over more of the company's management duties as his dad's health began to quickly deteriorate.

As a part of the management team, Roger believes one of his greatest achievements was the hiring of a new plant manager, Jim Bolin. Roger remembers that Senior Management was getting older at the time as most of his dad's Executive Team was around the same age as he was. Roger felt the company needed someone younger, but at the same time someone with experience.

> Roger Collins
> Son of George Collins Jr.
> Management
> 1977-1981
>
> *"Jim Bolin did wonders for our company."*

Roger continued to help manage Liberty after his dad's death in 1980. Meanwhile, Roger's older brother Fulton had returned to Oklahoma from California to focus on settling George Jr.'s estate. The original plan was for both brothers to run Liberty after their father's death, but that didn't turn out to be the case. The two quickly learned they had very different management styles.

> Roger Collins
> Son of George Collins Jr.
> Management
> 1977-1981
>
> *"There was clearly not room for both of us to be running the company at that stage of the game."*

At this time, Roger decided it was best for him to leave Liberty for his brother to run alone. Roger next tried his hand at a high-tech venture, which in his words "failed miserably".

As the Collins siblings divided their father's assets, Roger next turned his focus to another family business. While Fulton would now own and operate Liberty, Roger took over the Collins' oil and gas company.

> Roger Collins
> Son of George Collins Jr.
> Management
> 1977-1981
>
> *"I decided to take the oil and gas business. At the time I thought I was getting the better deal, but that was before oil and gas prices collapsed."*

Over the years, Roger proved to be a very successful businessman, adding Link America, a large trucking company, to his list of assets. He recently sold the business and today manages his own investments.

Roger and his wife Francy live in Tulsa, and even though it's been over 30 years since he came home to help run the family business, Roger Collins says he'll always remember his own link to Liberty Glass.

Chapter Five

If Only These Walls Could Talk
Inside the Liberty Glass Plant

If only these walls could talk. No doubt this phrase was repeated often at the Liberty Glass Plant. The work itself was all consuming, with long days, not to mention lonely nights, for those who were unlucky enough to work the graveyard shift.

In manufacturing, jobs are often described as monotonous and repetitive, but Liberty's employees do not seem to remember ever being bored.

It is also common in a manufacturing plant for work to be performed under the most challenging conditions, and at Liberty that was certainly the case in the hot-end. It was the hardest job in the plant, but it was also the one that paid the best wages.

Here in this huge melting pot, raw materials were heated to a boiling point in order to begin the process of making glass. The noise level in the hot-end was deafening and the conditions were smelly and dirty at best, but that wasn't the worst part. In the summer, temperatures in this area could reach up to 140 degrees. Employee Bill Oldham summed up the hot-end in very specific terms.

Bill Oldham
Moldmaker/Mold Shop Supervisor
1956-2000

"Noisy, smoky and dirty."

Pete Egan
Sapulpa Community Leader

"A lot of families worked at Liberty Glass. As a matter of fact, some of the old jokes are that Liberty Glass educated more kids from Sapulpa than any other company. The joke was that they went out there in the summertime and worked in the hot-end of the factory and then decided they did not want to do that anymore. Instead they were going to get an education."

Judge Rick Woolery
Judge of District Court
Sapulpa Community Leader
President, Sapulpa Historical Museum

"I remember as I got into high school and classmates talking about going to work there. Everybody talked about the hot-end and how hard the work was there, and I decided then that I would go study so I wouldn't have to work in the hot end."

Beverley Collins Ward
Daughter of George Collins Jr.

"My first memory of Liberty Glass is when I was a small girl, and Dad took me to his office to show it to me. The offices were nice, but what I especially remember were the buildings where they made the glass bottles. I was fascinated with the process, and will never forget the molten glass being pushed out of the furnaces in shape of the specific bottles. I admired the people who worked there as it was indeed very hot!"

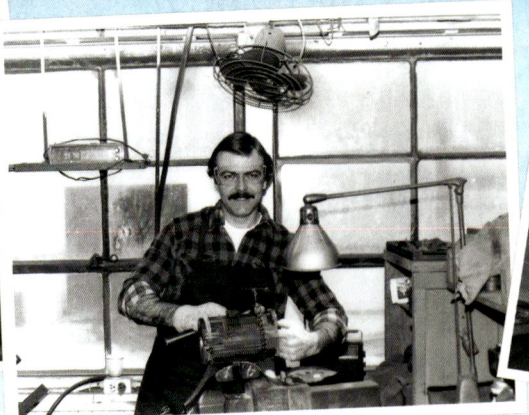

If the hot-end was too hot, then the warehouse was too cold. Gary Oyler worked in Inventory during part of his time at Liberty, and can still remember just how unbearably frigid the warehouse could be.

Gary Oyler
Service/Inventory/Payroll
1978-1994

"Sometimes you'd be so cold you'd be out in the warehouse and you'd be carrying a little calculator and you'd punch in the numbers and it would be so cold it wouldn't work. So you try to count them, write the pallets down and the number of bottles on each pallet and then you'd go back and do the math in the warmth. The west warehouse was the coldest place on earth. The wind would be blowing and the air would be coming through the aisles."

Liberty employees still recall that a laser-like focus was required for each individual job at the plant. One small slip-up and you could throw the entire system off balance, or worse, you could jeopardize your own safety or that of a co-worker's.

Bob Hill spent forty-two years at the plant, and says due to all the safety hazards, workers sometimes felt the need for prayer inside Liberty Glass. No doubt that's one of the reasons the company let Bob lead a daily devotional.

Bob Hill
Mold Shop
1956-1998

"The men in the mold shop were mostly spiritual people, and I've learned since then that's the only thing that counts."

Supervisors were constantly trying to improve safety conditions at Liberty, but as at any large manufacturing facility, injuries were inevitable.

Johnny Brison lost his finger at the plant, and in spite of a trip to the emergency room, he never got that finger back.

Johnny L. Brison
Plant Maintenance/
Plant Maintenance Supervisor
1959-1994

"I had been out there a long time and had no business doing what I did. The plant manager and I had gone out to lunch, and he wanted to look at a roof that was right over on top of the old decorating department. He thought it needed to be replaced. I just had on a pair of loafers and the two of us were up there looking at that roof. We got on one end and walked all the way to the other end. We had planned to go down a ladder, but when I stepped over to go down, my foot slipped out from under me because I had on those leather-soled shoes."

"Back then, all the roofs were put on with big lead-headed nails. When I fell I started to slide down that roof and unfortunately I was wearing a diamond ring that got caught on a nail and it just pulled that finger off. The plant manager was behind me and I looked around and told him to get my finger. And he said, 'I got it!' He had picked up my finger." (laughs)

"They did put it back on, but the next day they had to take it off because it didn't get any blood circulation."

Another employee injured on the job was Velma Littlefield, but unlike Johnny, her injury healed.

Velma Littlefield
Packing/ Lab/Box Shop/Label Machine
1955-1996

"I stepped off these boards that you walked on and the bottles fell over. I went around back to keep more from falling and to set some of them up, and I just stepped wrong."

"I knew it hurt. But I went ahead and worked the rest of my shift, and when I started to leave I told my supervisor, Coleman Rogers, that I had hurt my foot and was probably going to have to go to the doctor. So he wrote me an excuse and I went home and went to bed. They put it in a cast, and I was off work for a while."

Miss Ella Pepperkorn was honored Friday, February 28, 1969, when officials and employees of Liberty Glass Company, Tulsa-Sapulpa Union Railway, and Red Ball Truck Line gathered to congratulate her and wish her well upon her retirement after more than 26 years with the three associated companies.

Mr. George F. Collins, Jr., president of Liberty Glass, T.S.U., and Red Ball, Inc., presented Miss Pepperkorn with an engraved watch and a copy of the book, "Hawaii". At the time of her retirement on February 28, 1969, Miss Pepperkorn was employed as an Assistant Traffic Manager of Liberty Glass Company.

Pictured above with Miss Pepperkorn from left to right are: Mr. Frank Burzio, Secretary of both Tulsa-Sapulpa Union Railway Company and Red Ball, Inc.; Mr. Berry Rea, Traffic Assistant Manager of Liberty Glass Company; Mr. George F. Collins, Jr., and Mr. Ed Gosvener, Assistant Traffic Manager of Liberty Glass Company.

(Right) Employees pose for a 20th Anniversary photo.

Throughout the years, many people came to Liberty looking for a job, but often found themselves with a life-long career. Twenty, thirty, even forty years often seemed the norm.

Terry Kelley
Director of Purchasing/
Manager of Engineering Services
1965-1994

"My brother-in-law worked at Liberty Glass, and I was working construction at the time. He told me they were hiring, and I came over and filled out the application. They asked me if I could take a physical the next day and I did, then they told me to come back out to the plant. Then they asked me if I could go to work on Monday, which I did."

"I had no idea I'd still be there 30 years later. I was 19 at the time, and we had a one month old baby."

Glenn F. Nix
Supervisor
Maintenance, Batch & Furnace
1953-1994

"When I went there, I was only going to work for a short while and then quit. I was just going to work long enough to make me a little money and I got caught, I stayed."

Glenn came to the plant in 1953 and was still there the day Liberty sold, 41 years later.

Surprisingly, Glen was not the record holder for length of employment at Liberty. That honor belonged to Harold Hinderer in Payroll, who worked at the company for 50 years.

Gary Oyler
Service/Inventory/Payroll
1978-1994

"He was the only one that made it 50 years. The company gave him a watch."

Why did so many employees stay for so many years? The reasons varied. Most liked living in Sapulpa and did not want to leave, but there was also this. Liberty Glass was a very good job with very good pay and equally as important, employees also felt they were truly appreciated.

Bill Oldham
Moldmaker/Mold Shop Supervisor
1956-2000

"George Collins Jr. had a tremendous feeling for his working people. Also you came to realize he was a fair man. He was also a very good businessman."

"One of the things you realized over the years is that first of all, Liberty was known for its quality."

Bob Hill
Mold Shop
1956-1998

"We were there because they treated us right."

Perhaps even more importantly, there was a great sense of pride among employees. Working side by side, day after day, year after year, lives woven together for a long period of time brought a unique intimacy to the group. There was a brotherhood and a sisterhood all sharing the pride of a job well done.

Johnny L. Brison
Plant Maintenance/
Plant Maintenance Supervisor
1959-1994

"It was a good place to work. It was a lot of fun and you know you just had something to do and everybody did what they were supposed to do."

Bob Hill
Mold Shop
1956-1998

"They all made an effort to do right and to do their job properly."

Liberty employees also took pride in knowing their company had long been considered a leader in the glass industry. There were many examples to justify this standing. In 1920, the Sapulpa Herald reported that Liberty was the only plant west of the Mississippi making milk bottles.

If Only These Walls Could Talk - Inside the Liberty Glass Plant

A Preview of LIBERTY'S ECONOTAINER

Another achievement of note that came later was the Enconotainer, which Liberty introduced during the early 1940's. It was a square-shaped, flint glass reusable milk bottle. Among its many advantages over the old round type bottle were large savings in space and weight.

In 1948, Liberty Glass again made history when they developed the world's first multi-color process called "LUSTROCOLOR". It was a method of fusing color pigments into glass surfaces, and customers could choose from a variety of 12 different colors in any combination. Furthermore, the labels and artwork could be applied to all four sides or panels of the bottle. This process revolutionized the color decoration of glass products worldwide.

Only one of these prototype bottles still exists today, and Les Hughes donated it to the Sapulpa Historical Museum. It is one-of-a-kind, and the last remaining example of the Liberty Glass Company's prototype bottle that made glass history.

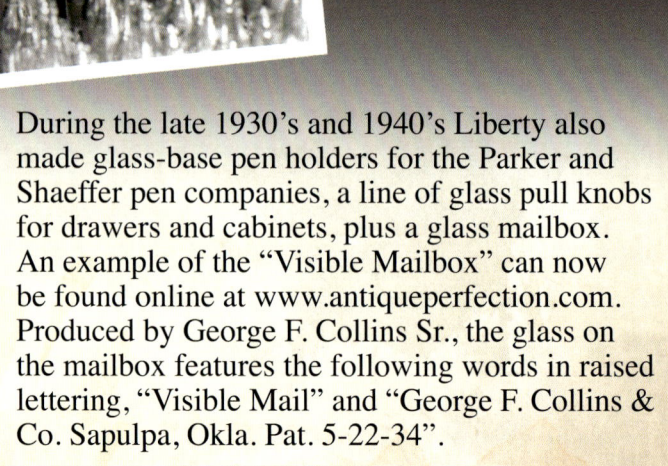

During the late 1930's and 1940's Liberty also made glass-base pen holders for the Parker and Shaeffer pen companies, a line of glass pull knobs for drawers and cabinets, plus a glass mailbox. An example of the "Visible Mailbox" can now be found online at www.antiqueperfection.com. Produced by George F. Collins Sr., the glass on the mailbox features the following words in raised lettering, "Visible Mail" and "George F. Collins & Co. Sapulpa, Okla. Pat. 5-22-34".

In addition to sharing life inside the Liberty Plant, employees shared their lives in the world outside. Punching time cards as they came to work, each person carried into the plant all the good and bad that came with their lives. Kathy Wilson, who worked as the plant's switchboard operator, says management recognized employees were also people with concerns and responsibilities apart from their work.

Kathy Wilson
Plant Switchboard Operator
Secretary to Fulton Collins
1988-1995

"When I started work at Liberty, my daughter was 10 months old, so she was pretty small. It was no problem at all if either of the kids were sick, no problem at all. You called in and if you told them your child was sick, they would say, 'Okay, see you tomorrow'. They were very kind and understanding and helpful in those areas."

Some came to Liberty right out of high school and did not leave until the day they retired. Over the years, babies were born and grandparents buried. There were birthdays celebrated and holidays shared. Sometimes the guys in the plant would use their skills to make gifts for their co-workers, one of those being a glass bottle made in honor of Harold Hinderer's retirement party. Co-worker Gary Oyler remembers the gift was designed to recognize Harold's unprecedented 50 years of service.

Gary Oyler
Service/Inventory/Payroll
1978-1994

*"When Harold Hinderer retired they took one of the real thin glass bottles they were making the last few years in Emerald green and put his name in the side of a mold and produced some bottles. It had **Harold Hinderer, Fifty Years**."*

50 years
Harold Hinderer

If Only These Walls Could Talk - Inside the Liberty Glass Plant

Over the years, Harold was not the only one who received a unique gift made in the factory. Velma Littlefield and Catherine Williams recall some of the other special items crafted in the plant.

Velma Littlefield Packing/ Lab/Box Shop/Label Machine 1955-1996	*"Sometimes around Christmas they would play around down there, making ashtrays or whatever."*
Catherine L. Williams Packing and Checking 1958-1983	*"I have a Coke bottle they cut across. I use it for my pens and things like that. It's sitting right there on my desk."*

Sometimes the plant seemed like a small town all on its own. Everybody knew his neighbors, and gossip was whispered back and forth as stories would travel from one end of the plant to the other.

The guys at Liberty loved practical jokes and playing pranks on each other. When the supervisor turned his back, Bill Oldham remembers the weapons of choice were often water pistols or rubber band sling shots.

Bill Oldham Moldmaker/Mold Shop Supervisor 1956-2000	*"There are a ton of stories."* *"I should have been fired a hundred times before I became a Christian."* *"I remember the day I brought the water pistol out there. A lot of times we didn't do anything out in the open….we'd be sneaky."* *"I wasn't mean. I was mischievous and liked to cut up."*

However, as Bill Oldham will tell you, the same co-worker you pranked one week might be the one you consoled through tears and a time of sorrow the next week.

For the most part everyone seemed to get along at the plant, but sometimes heated arguments could be heard as co-workers shouted over the noise of the machinery.

As in any small town, these arguments could erupt at any given moment. The topics varied. Sometimes it was merely a difference of opinion, possibly over sports. Occasionally even politics entered the picture.

Bill Oldham
Moldmaker/Mold Shop Supervisor
1956-2000

"We did argue about politics. We did discuss those things, and we'd argue about who was running for President."

In some areas of the plant radios were allowed, giving workers the opportunity to follow and share in the world outside. If it was a weekend shift, some might be listening to an OU football game, or on Sundays the Dallas Cowboys were likely a favorite.

Perhaps some radios were tuned in to news programs and employees could have heard that World War II had ended or later that American Neil Armstrong walked on the moon or, sadly, that the country's President had been shot and later died in Dallas. At the plant, life marched on inside and out.

Bob Hill
Mold Shop
1956-1998

"We didn't always like what was going on in the world."

In the 1960's, what was going on in the world was Vietnam. Liberty's men and women recall the war hovering over their heads like a cloud. For Tom Syrles, a 19 year old from Muskogee, Vietnam was a very real and very personal concern.

Tom Syrles
Shipping Manager/Traffic Manager
1966-1990

"I was living in Muskogee and my grandparents happened to live here in Sapulpa, and I needed a summer job. I was going to school at Northeastern in Tahlequah. It was back during the Vietnam War, and I had actually joined the Army Reserve unit in Muskogee. During the time I was working at Liberty that summer, I found out I was going to have to leave and go to six month basic training. I would not be able to go back to college that next fall, because the training was going to interrupt that. I would not be finished until sometime in January, so I did not go back to college, I just continued to work."

"I worked out on the docks in shipping that summer before I went into the Guard. We were hand-loading everything. We were hand-loading trucks, and we had a day crew and an evening crew. It was pretty tough."

"There were some guys who worked out there who actually got drafted. They had to leave for the service, and some did not come back."

Tom returned to the plant after his six month Guard service, and didn't leave again until 1990, 24 years after he came looking for just a summer job.

Tom Syrles
Shipping Manager/Traffic Manager
1966-1990

"The plan was that I was just going to work that summer and go back to school. I went back to work and you know how it is, you get into making a little money and you have some obligations on buying a car and a few things, and I didn't go back to school."

Throughout his career, Tom proved to be one of the plant's most effective employees and for his efforts was promoted frequently, ultimately landing a supervisory role.

Tom Syrles
Shipping Manager/Traffic Manager
1966-1990

"That's the best thing that Liberty Glass gave me, they educated me. They educated me in what I wanted to do. I loved that end of the plant, the shipping, the warehousing, the transportation, and I asked for a couple of areas when openings came up [and got promoted]."

As one can imagine, there were many memorable events at Liberty. Some, like Tom Syrles, who received numerous promotions, remember their best days, while others say they'll never forget their worst. Johnny Brison is one of those.

> Johnny L. Brison
> Plant Maintenance/
> Plant Maintenance Supervisor
> 1959-1994

"February of 1978, Hell moved into that glass plant. And if you show me one person that worked out there at that point in time that tells you different, I tell you that guy is the dumbest guy that ever was to live."

That was the day Jim Bolin walked into Liberty Glass for the very first time. He was a large man, some say larger than life. Hired by the Collins family to oversee plant operations, Roger Collins, who was working in management at the time, felt Jim Bolin was just what the company needed.

> Roger Collins
> Son of George Collins Jr.
> Management
> 1977-1981

"Jim came in and really put in good cost controls in the plant…I think we had become a little lax, and he really put in some discipline and controls that really helped us at that stage of the game."

If Only These Walls Could Talk - Inside the Liberty Glass Plant

Terry Kelley
Director of Purchasing/
Manager of Engineering Services
1965-1994

"Jim Bolin had a big effect on my work there. He and I used to argue a lot in our meetings. He was on the company side, and I was on the union side. So we got to know each other pretty well. He asked me to be a supervisor and we had a little understanding that he wouldn't terminate me as soon as I got that job." (laughs)

"He saw something in me, I guess. He was basically the reason I progressed through whatever progression I did out there. I enjoyed working, and I just tried to do the best I could. I gave him what he wanted most of the time, I think."

"Jim was a good guy. He was a forceful person, and he'd say 'This is what I want'. And this is what I told him, 'I can't do the job if I don't know what you want'. If you didn't do the job, he wasn't bashful about telling you about it. Really, that's what you want or you can't get any better. 'If you need some help tell me'. The guy had a mind on him that you just don't see."

"Jim had an office at the plant, and he would never object to you walking into his office to talk for a minute. He would let you do your job. I guess that was one of the best things I liked about him. He didn't interfere, but if he had something to tell you he wasn't bashful about it either. He's probably one of the best people I've ever worked for. You just don't see a lot of people like that."

Margaret A. Fuller
Sales/Plant Manager's Secretary
1968-1974
1976-1994

"Jim Bolin was neat for me. I really liked him, he was good, and if I wanted to tell him something, he would say, 'Now Margaret wait a minute'."

"Not everybody liked him, but he was really good and he knew what he was doing."

Without question, Jim Bolin was a polarizing figure at Liberty Glass. To some he was the good guy in the white hat, but others were certain he was the bad guy in the black hat. Just the sight of him charging through the plant could make grown men quiver and department heads quake.

Hired out of Georgia, Jim Bolin was an unknown to the people of Liberty…a new man, and with him came a whole new way of doing things. Most agree Liberty needed change at the time, as the health of George Jr. was failing and, as a result, the company was struggling as well.

Jim Bolin
Plant Manager/President
1977-1994

"It really presented itself as a challenge, but they reassured me that I could have what I needed to do the job, and that turned out to be quite extensive after a short period of time."

"One of the first things I discovered was that we were totally over-manned. It was union controlled, and there were more people in there costing money than there were doing the work."

"My first trip through the factory, and I used to come back on every shift, there were at least five card games going on, not in the break area, but out in the plant where they had tables set up. As Frank Collins told me, 'It's awful. You've got a lot of people problems.' And he was right. That was the first thing that was totally obvious. The second thing was the state of repair. The plant was in pretty poor shape."

"I was very unpopular. I brought the union in and we sat down at a table and I told them what I saw. I told them every time I found a card game, wherever it was, I was going to lay off four people because that was four we didn't need that were playing cards. I think that first two weeks I laid off 86 people who were playing cards."

"It was a tough thing. They brought in the international union and they understood there was a problem. All the union officials did. They never once said that what we were doing didn't need to be done."

With Jim Bolin now in the driver's seat, expectations and standards in almost every category reached a new high. Terry Kelley says one of the most important things Jim did was to insist on a better work ethic, a goal Kelley says he embraced himself.

Terry Kelley
Director of Purchasing/
Manager of Engineering Services
1965-1994

"I knew what he was looking for in an employee. I tried to do the same thing when I hired a person…to get people that were there for more than just the pay and to go home. They had pride about what they were doing and the things they offered in their work. It's good when you have people that come in and tell you things that you want to know before you ask for them. That's what you want. You know then that they're doing their job."

"The thing is, I always felt that if you set your standards high enough, then you wouldn't have any problems from your boss. You should always set your standards higher than your boss."

In addition to the 86 people Jim fired for playing cards, he laid off hundreds more for various other reasons.

Jim Bolin
Plant Manager/President
1977-1994

"If I remember …994 or something like that. We ended up with a work force of 400…432, actually."

As a result, Liberty's bottom line was impacted very quickly under Jim Bolin. In August of 1978, a little over six months after he arrived, the company made $1.3 million.

Jim Bolin
Plant Manager/President
1977-1994

"There was still more that could be done, but that happened to be the right mix at the right time. The equipment was not there to be able to make nonreturnable small ware and make a profit on it because the glass accounting system is based off cost per ton of glass. So if you are going to make a cheaper product at a lighter weight, then you've got to run a greater speed to get the same cost per ton."

David Beyer
Accounting Department
Chief Financial Officer
1972-1994

"Part of the reason we needed Jim's skills was that for a long period of time we were a returnable production company. The pricing was very good and returnable bottles are easier to produce than non- returnable, and the industry had to make the shift to more and more non-returnable, where the prices are less. However, the bottles are more difficult to make because they are lighter weight. We did not get the expertise in there soon enough to make that change."

Based on past experience, Jim Bolin knew exactly what to do. Having been through this change at his previous employer's, Jim quickly realized that for Liberty to be successful, the company would have to re-tool its strategy, its equipment and its people.

One of those who worked closely with Jim in upgrading Liberty's equipment was ironworker David Bennett, who specialized in rebuilding furnaces. Bolin and Bennett had become friends when they previously worked together in Georgia, and after assessing the dilapidated plant at Liberty, Bolin called on his old friend for help.

David Bennett
Owner Bennett Steel/Liberty Construction
1980-Present

"I told him, 'I don't have the money to start a business and fund workers' comp and liability insurance.' He told me to just come talk to him."

"He said he would advance me the money and I could start a business and work it off. I asked if he was really willing to do that, and he said he was absolutely willing to do that for me."

"That's how Bennett Steel got started. It was off that $50,000 advance that Liberty Glass gave me back in 1980."

"If Jim liked you, if he had confidence in you, you never did worry if he had your back or not. Jim always valued people that were dependable."

If Only These Walls Could Talk - Inside the Liberty Glass Plant

Of course, not everyone liked Jim Bolin the way David Bennett did, particularly at first. As we know, with change often comes resentment, especially with so many people losing their jobs and others having to retrain for all the new skills needed at the plant.

Jim Bolin
Plant Manager/President
1977-1994

"I fought change both within the plant and outside it. I used to tell everybody to stand your ground. If you think I'm wrong, tell me. If you believe you're right, then you've got to stand your ground."

As he made his daily walk-throughs at the plant, Bolin says he could clearly feel the undercurrent of resentment, and often times he could also hear it.

Terry Kelley
Director of Purchasing/
Manager of Engineering Services
1965-1994

"A lot of guys were afraid of him."

"We had some guys in our union who would not have cared if Jesus Christ had been there, they would not have liked him because he's the Plant Manager. That was the attitude and that had to change and that did change."

As time passed and the company started to make money, more and more people began to understand and appreciate all the things Jim Bolin had done to make Liberty a success.

David Beyer
Accounting Department
Chief Financial Officer
1972-1994

"I am at this meeting. Jim's going all around the room and talking to his department heads. One guy had a problem that Jim did not like. Jim told us he was going to explode and blow up through the roof and I was looking for him to go. I was convinced."

"The point being, he was passionate and therefore people became passionate about doing well, and that was a win-win. As time went on, respect is all that really matters, and Jim had their respect."

Glen F. Nix
Supervisor
Maintenance, Batch and Furnace
1953-1994

"I would say he saved the glass plant, but he was a holy terror."

Anonymous

"I got along with him all right, but he was not one of my favorite people. You ain't gonna' put that in the book, are you?"

Even Johnny Brison admits he now realizes Jim Bolin was only trying to do what he felt was necessary for the company to succeed.

Johnny L. Brison
Plant Maintenance/
Plant Maintenance Supervisor
1959-1994

"He was probably the meanest guy I ever knew, but he saved the glass plant. If it had not been for him, there wouldn't be a Liberty Glass. Jim saved the plant because George was losing so much money he was thinking about shutting it down."

"We were trying to break into beer bottles. We were losing three or four cents per bottle making Coors bottles."

"Jim put in a new compressor room. He wasn't in there a month before he started putting in everything new. He redesigned that whole world out there."

"Jim was a smart man, but he had an opinionated personality to him. I guess he had to be that way to survive."

Roger Collins
Son of George Collins Jr.
Management
1977-1981

"Two liter plastic came in 1978 and wiped out about 30% of our market share. Jim Bolin and our marketing team came up with the idea of light weight glass bottles with paper labels. We then licensed that technology to others so it would have better customer penetration."

Once Jim Bolin put his plans for Liberty into action, things improved for the company; however, the best news of all was still to come. It came in the form of Liberty's brightest, most talented leader to date. After the death of his father, Fulton Collins made the decision to come home to Oklahoma, and most importantly home to Liberty Glass.

If Only These Walls Could Talk - Inside the Liberty Glass Plant

Chapter Six

The First Family of *Liberty Glass*
Part 3

No leader in the history of Liberty Glass came into the company with the talent, skills and qualifications of Fulton Collins.

George F. Collins, III (Fulton)

Chief Executive Officer
1980-1994

The oldest son of George Jr. and Beverly Collins, Fulton attended preparatory school on the East Coast, and next moved west to Stanford, where he earned his Bachelor's Degree in Economics in 1965, his MBA in 1967 and, one year later, his Masters of Science in Operations Research.

After Stanford Fulton stayed in California and, from 1971 to 1980, served as Group Vice President of a biotechnology and pharmaceutical company, Syntex Corporation. Fulton was highly regarded at Syntex, where his knowledge and leadership skills became apparent early in his career.

Syntex is also where he met his future wife, Susie McCabe. She was a teacher from Iowa who had relocated to the West Coast and was working at a temporary job at Syntex until she could find a teaching position. The couple married in 1977. Fulton had two children from a previous marriage, George F. Collins IV, known as Fulty, and daughter Carolyn. Susie and Fulton would later add two more daughters to the family, Suzanne and Chrissy. Both girls grew up in Tulsa, where the couple had moved in 1981.

Susie says Fulton was drawn back to his Oklahoma roots after his father's death, but it was not an easy decision. Fulton and his siblings, Beverley and Roger, inherited Liberty Glass, but Fulton already had a very promising career with Syntex. In fact, he was one of those being groomed for the company's Presidency. But Liberty needed help. Fulton was committed to first try to save the company, and then sell it to ensure the financial future of his family and his siblings.

Jim Bolin
Plant Manager/President
1977-1994

"When Fulton first came, his plan was to liquidate Liberty Glass and shut it down. He actually told me that. So I went and found David Beyer and told him we needed to put together a proposal to show Fulton what we've come through. We had just put in a compressor system, and that was a bad year. And we put together a performa of what we could do and where we could go."

Susie Collins
Wife of Fulton Collins

"It was a surprise when his father died that October. We thought we were staying in California for a long time. We had no intention of moving back to Tulsa, so when we came back, it was to settle his father's estate and to sell the company."

"It took two years for him to settle the estate. By then we had become involved in the community, and Fulton loved being with his brothers. We both liked Tulsa and both loved the people."

Based on what he learned from Jim Bolin and David Beyer's proposal, Fulton turned his attention to the vision they had outlined.

From all indications, Liberty was now poised to enter a new era. With cash in the bank from their father's estate, Fulton and Roger planned to grow the struggling business together. The brothers had purchased their sister Beverley's portion of the company once the estate was settled.

Finally, it seemed things might calm down at Liberty, but that didn't turn out to be the case.

Roger Collins
Son of George Collins Jr.
Management
1977-1981

"My brother and I really didn't see eye to eye on how to run a business."

Roger said he favored a looser management style, while his brother's was more structured and required more accountability from employees.

Because of their differences, Roger decided it was best for him to leave Liberty.

Fulton's leadership assets proved crucial to the company, a fact that was recognized by almost everyone. In addition to being extremely bright, he also embraced new ideas in technology and glassmaking, and he was willing to take risks, while at the same time keeping a close eye on the company's bottom line.

As the proliferation of plastics in the soda industry continued, smaller size bottles became popular. Assessing the situation, Fulton soon realized Liberty needed to transition into the business of manufacturing beer bottles. He also saw the importance of developing a faster bottle making machine. Time and again, Fulton proved he was never afraid to spend money if he knew his investment would make money.

PALLET LOADS OF GLASS IN GAYLORD BOXES AWAIT PROCESSING IN LIBERTY'S CULLET HANDLING SYSTEM.

Susie Collins
Wife of Fulton Collins

"He loved the business challenge."

Fulton Collins IV
Son of Fulton Collins

"I would describe him first as an academic. He thrived on learning, and for him everything was an academic exercise. Everything had a solution. It's like he would say, 'That's a problem that has a solution, so I need to take this step, then this step, then this step to solve this problem'. In terms of being a leader, I can say emphatically he was knowledgeable about any topic he was talking about. And if he wasn't, he would ask questions and do the reading and research until he had gained that knowledge."

"When you talk about leadership style he was not the type of guy who wanted to get up and give speeches and motivate people in that way. That was not him at all. He was much more into working collaboratively, with a person, and gaining the knowledge he needed. A perfect example was his working relationship with Jim Bolin. Dad knew Jim was the expert at making glass bottles in the plant, and also on the operations end. Dad respected him for that, and he learned everything he could from him, and then when Dad had a conversation with Jim he could have it more as an equal."

MARGARET FULLER TAKES THE FIRST STEP IN GLASS RECYCLING.

Fulton Collins IV
Son of Fulton Collins

"Dad gained respect from the people he worked with by his academic prowess. People always knew he was a very thoughtful person and genuinely cared. He made hard decisions, but he genuinely cared and was concerned about the people in the company."

"Socially he was outgoing, but he was also shy. It was never about him, it was more about Liberty Glass. He did not thrive on attention, and he did not need attention to validate himself as a leader."

Jim Bolin
Plant Manager/President
1977-1994

"Fulton was very fair. He was a quiet leader. He would sit down and explain problems, even if he did not know the solution. He was very, very bright financially. He knew what he wanted and he expected you to tell him how to get there."

David Beyer
Accounting Department
Chief Financial Officer
1972-1994

"He was a better CPA than I was, which is why I learned very quickly to say, 'I don't know'. He respected that. If you couldn't answer his question it was best to tell him that you didn't know, but that you would find out."

"On one occasion, we went to meet with the attorneys. We had a 30-page document outlining the 401(k) plan. Essentially I had read it and written some notes, but other people had not read it. Fulton had not been there that long, and people were not yet used to working with him. He made it very clear in that meeting, 'Do not ever come to another meeting unprepared. If you don't know you don't know, but be prepared. Work hard, be honest, and be prepared'. You had the tools, the authority, the accountability to do your job, but you had to plan, and you had to tell him what you were doing."

"The first time we had to do a major refinancing of the company, I didn't know how to do that. That's what Fulton had done at Syntex. Fulton did the whole process, and when he finished he told me that's how he wanted me to do it next time. We did several refinancing jobs, and we spent a lot of money in the plant. There would be times we would have to borrow quite a bit of money to do that and take that risk. Other than keeping him advised, he let me run with it. He took the time to train me and then let me run with it."

David Beyer
Accounting Department
Chief Financial Officer
1972-1994

"Basically, after Fulton trusted you, all you had to do was tell him what you needed, but you still had to do the paperwork to follow up."

David Block
IT Department Manager
1967-1994

"Fulton was a genius. He really encouraged us to move forward."

Vickie Varnell Beyer
Accounting Department/
Fulton Collins Secretary during Strike
1974-1976
1983-1990

"Fulton was very, very confident on top of being very intelligent. He knew how smart he was and he was very confident about it, but he also was confident enough that he never hesitated about bringing in expertise where he wasn't an expert. He definitely knew how to hire the best. He knew where his strengths were and how to build a team."

Kathy Wilson
Switchboard Operator/
Secretary to Fulton Collins
1988-1995

"There were some days when he was maybe more business-like than others. He was never a big joker. He was real on-the-job while he was here. I just respected him so much and thought he was so smart."

Michael K. Wille
Assistant Controller/Plant Controller
1974-1989

"Fulton had a way of making you feel very, very comfortable. He realized he was a very intelligent fellow, but he never carried himself like that or had to let you know how intelligent he was. His actions spoke obviously."

Bob Hall, who for years owned the truck stop and café near the plant, had a close relationship with Fulton. Bob says the two often had long and interesting conversations about a wide variety of topics, most of them relating to Liberty Glass.

Bob Hall
Truck Stop and Café Owner
1952-2000

"When Mr. Collins died and Fulton inherited the company, he told me one day he'd spent $45 million remodeling the plant, and it sure changed the looks of things. He also told me that they were shipping 40 carloads of glass a day."

"Another time Fulton called and asked me to come down and talk to him. He wanted to know that when I was younger what would be the first thing I saw when I would drive from Tulsa to Sapulpa at night. I told him it was that big LG up there. It was lit up then, and it was our landmark, and he said he was going to fix that thing and light it up again. And he did. One of the guys that worked down at the plant told me that he wished I would quit giving Fulton ideas, because it always meant more work."

Almost everyone who knew Fulton Collins considered him a genius, but Susie Collins, agreeing with Mike Wille's assessment, says Fulton never thought of himself in those terms.

Susie Collins
Wife of Fulton Collins

"I would not call him a genius, and he never thought of himself as one. He said the genius was the guy who lived across the hall from him at Andover Preparatory School who got a perfect score on his SAT test."

"He always felt there were other people out there who were smarter than he was. He said the smartest guy he ever met was George Kaiser."

"Fulton was very bright, and I used to wonder where he got all that knowledge… He never read novels, I never saw him read books. He read numerous newspapers and just seemed to absorb information so quickly. I just loved his mind."

"He was very humble, shy actually, in many respects. I don't think he had any idea how truly gifted he was."

Fulton's humility is clearly illustrated in his reaction to the number of automobiles the company owned when he first came to Liberty. According to Susie, George Jr. had a fleet of cars including a limousine which embarrassed Fulton, and he immediately sold them once he assumed leadership.

Robert Lorton Jr.
Brother of Fulton Collins
Plant Worker
1953-1954

"Fulton once told me his style of management was "the walk around" kind. Meaning he was out in the shop… keeping track of what was going on, talking to everybody. His intellect was such that he was a natural leader. He was always on top of everything and had exceptional vision."

Over the years, Fulton's leadership would prove instrumental in Liberty's eventual rise to the top of the glass industry, but of course he didn't do it alone.

Like his father and grandfather before him, Fulton depended heavily on the people of Liberty Glass. He knew well how valuable the work of each and every department would be as he ushered the company into the future.

The First Family of Liberty Glass - Part 3

Chapter Seven

The Departments of *Liberty Glass*

Liberty Glass consisted of a number of key departments, all combining to provide the skills and expertise needed to operate a large-scale glass business. As in any well-oiled machine, it was imperative that the company's individual parts work together in harmony as one cohesive unit. Liberty executives knew that teamwork was an integral component in the complex environment of glass making, and that a better product resulted when a team approach was taken.

In addition to plant personnel and the executive staff, Liberty's team consisted of Accounting, Sales and IT Departments.

WORELL DEES

The life-blood of any manufacturer is the sale of hi[s product]. As Assistant Sales Manager and as Coordinator of Scheduling [and] Shipping, Worell Dees works closely with various departme[nts and] Liberty Customers in scheduling the steady outflow of Lib[erty Glass].

Worell started with the company in 1935 as a constr[uction worker]. From that foothold he began his steady advancement, fir[st as a] screen mounting department to the position of inventory [clerk, then as] Supervisor of the Order Department, which position he h[eld until] promoted to his present capacity.

A member of the Church of the Nazarene and a graduate of Sapulpa schools, Worell lists as his hobbies—cycling, bee keeping and gardening.

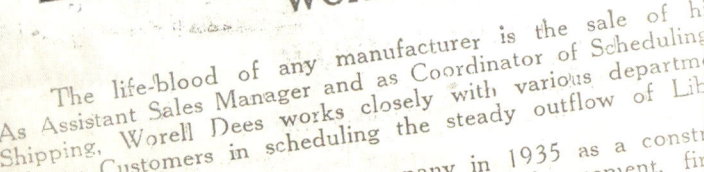

*"A **Sales Service** offered in a **Spirit of Cooperation** and **Friendliness**."*

Accounting
The Accounting Department

The Accounting Department in any company is vital to the business's overall success, but especially so in manufacturing. Liberty Glass was fortunate to have an excellent department, and most agree that one of the primary reasons was David Beyer, who came to the company in 1972.

David Beyer
Accounting Department
Chief Financial Officer
1972-1994

"I was hired by the Treasurer, Bob Fisher. My title was "Assistant to the Treasurer."

"My first day at work, I saw the little movie. It was the story of Liberty Glass, and it was called I am Glass, and that was my orientation."

"I had been in the Tulsa area since 1968, with Price Waterhouse. The reason I was looking for a job was the Price Waterhouse office in Tulsa was closing, and I could either transfer to Dallas or transfer to Nashville. I had recently gotten married and I did not want to move. I looked around for some jobs, and that's where I ended up."

David Beyer went on to serve as Liberty's Controller and later Treasurer, then, thanks to his outstanding job performance, was eventually promoted to Chief Financial Officer.

David was not only an accomplished accountant, he was also very good at personnel decisions, and over the years he made some very important hires in his department.

One of those was Michael Wille, a graduate of the University of Tulsa who came on board in 1974. Michael was a small-town boy from Illinois and says he thinks that was one of the key factors in David Beyer offering him a job.

Michael K. Wille
Accounting Department
Assistant Controller/Plant Controller
1974-1989

"The reason I think I really got the job was that I'm originally from Illinois, and David is from Illinois. He's a farm boy, and he told me to always have the mentality of a farmer. The weather's the only thing you have to worry about, and you can't do anything about that."

The Departments of Liberty Glass

David Beyer was serving as Controller at the time he hired Mike Wille. The existing Treasurer, Bob Fisher, had just passed away, and it was expected that David would be promoted to Treasurer and Mike would replace David as Controller. Surprisingly, things didn't quite work out that way.

Michael K. Wille
Accounting Department
Assistant Controller/Plant Controller
1974-1989

"At the same time David Beyer hired me, George Collins hired Wayne Weese as Treasurer."

"Now all of a sudden we had three people in two positions. My initial response was it was kind of nice, because all of a sudden you had the work split. We had the work split three ways instead of two."

"What was really kind of exciting, this was back in 1974, was that all the record keeping, except for payroll, everything was manual in the company. I got the opportunity to work with one of the nerds, David Block (laugh), and we basically walked through the systems and got to automate accounting systems, payable systems, all through the systems. It was a neat challenge to start that up from scratch and automate all the systems."

Another significant hire made by David Beyer was Bruce Ryan, an experienced glass industry accountant who came to Liberty in 1982.

Working in Warner Robbins, Georgia, Bruce heard about an opening in Liberty's Accounting Department through an acquaintance. After applying, he got an offer from David Beyer, but initially turned the job down. Obviously impressed by Bruce's qualifications, David was persistent and offered him the job again.

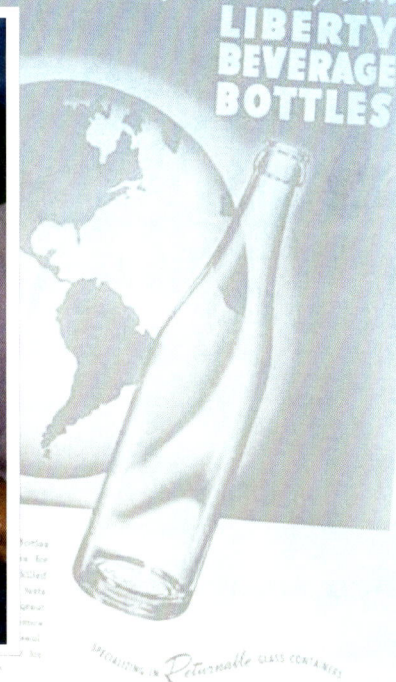

R. Bruce Ryan
Accounting Department
Plant Accountant/Assistant Controller/
Controller
1982-1992

"The second time he called me I knew I had him and I could name my price."

Michael K. Wille
Accounting Department
Assistant Controller/Plant Controller
1974-1989

"The good thing about Bruce was that he had a lot of experience in the glass industry and in dealing with the strong-willed folks, let's say, at times."

"Bruce was able to step in and just realize from the get-go what to expect from that perspective."

"He obviously had some great background in the glass industry and manufacturing side of it as plant controller."

R. Bruce Ryan
Accounting Department
Plant Accountant/Assistant Controller/
Controller
1982-1992

"One of the major things I brought with me was a relationship with Jim Bolin, whom I had met back at the other glass company in Georgia."

Bruce says one thing he learned about Jim at the previous company was that the plant manager did not like accountants coming into his area of the plant asking questions, snooping around and basically wondering how much money Jim was spending or why he had approved certain expenditures.

> R. Bruce Ryan
> Accounting Department
> Plant Accountant/Assistant Controller/
> Controller
> 1982-1992
>
> *"He really didn't like people looking over his shoulder, and I was a persistent little rascal. I was going to get the information no matter what."*
>
> *"Jim could be a very intimidating individual when he wanted to be, and he had a very unique way of testing you. As a matter of fact, I'm going to tell a story."*

Bruce found out how "unique" Jim Bolin's way of testing someone could be from a very personal experience. As Bruce tells it, one day he and Jim happened to be passing each other in a very narrow passageway at the plant in Georgia. As the two men came face to face, Jim Bolin shockingly took a swing at the accountant. Bruce didn't flinch, but calmly ducked out of the way, didn't say a word and just kept on walking. It was Jim's way of testing Bruce, and from that moment on he knew he couldn't intimidate the mild-mannered accountant.

> R. Bruce Ryan
> Accounting Department
> Plant Accountant/Assistant Controller/
> Controller
> 1982-1992
>
> *"We actually became friends. Still are."*

Today Bruce Ryan laughs as he tells the story, and no doubt his calm approach in dealing with Jim Bolin paved the way for a better relationship between Liberty's Accounting Department and the Plant Manager - ultimately leading to improved operations.

> Jim Bolin
> Plant Manager/President
> 1977-1994
>
> *"I can tell you how it happened. I asked for costs and I wanted to see the cost sheets so I could see what we're doing and they didn't have any."*

> David Beyer
> Accounting Department
> Chief Financial Officer
> 1972-1994
>
> *"Nobody looked at them. We had information, but the structure wasn't there where anybody looked at them like they should."*
>
> *"When Jim came, he asked why he didn't have this stuff. The expectation not only from Jim, but then ultimately from all our department heads changed over time. They started wanting to know what their costs were so they could run their department properly."*
>
> *"We had good quality people, but the expectations weren't there to drive it."*

Bruce Ryan insists high expectations and tough questions are necessary factors in glass industry accounting.

R. Bruce Ryan
Accounting Department
Plant Accountant/Assistant Controller/
Controller
1982-1992

"I like to dig down into what makes a glass plant run. From the moment the raw materials come through the back door to when they go to the furnace, hit the forming machines, go through cooling, get packaged and go out the door."

"I want to know every step of that process. What makes it tick? How does it affect the financial statements? What do I need to be looking for?"

One of the Accounting Department's responsibilities at Liberty was to help develop cost-saving ideas, and then, once those ideas were implemented, they were asked to measure their cost-effectiveness.

One such example was when Jim Bolin and Wills Young led Liberty in introducing a new soft drink bottle concept. They proposed a plain, single glass bottle with a label attached to it, as opposed to the old decorated bottles.

The Departments of Liberty Glass

Michael Wille noticed an immediate problem with the cost effectiveness of the new bottle, as the product was costing double what the company had budgeted.

> Michael K. Wille
> Accounting Department
> Assistant Controller/Plant Controller
> 1974-1989
>
> *"I was watching the cost control and was supposed to be monitoring the glue used to attach the labels. Somebody had cranked up the applicator on that thing and it was putting way too much glue on the bottles. They were putting three times the glue on it."*

After that Jim Bolin even went so far as to increase the frequency of the Accounting Department's cost reporting. The plant manager vowed this kind of problem would not happen again, at least not while he was in charge.

> Michael K. Wille
> Accounting Department
> Assistant Controller/Plant Controller
> 1974-1989
>
> *"Before Jim we would do monthly cost reporting, which would come out three months after the end of the month. So like the January report would show up in April. These would be the most beautiful reports on pristine paper, but totally worthless because they were three months late. When Bolin came in we had weekly costing."*

It might be safe to assume that Jim Bolin never did learn to like snoopy accountants asking him questions. Or maybe he just learned to live with it out of his respect for Bruce Ryan or his appreciation of the astuteness Michael Wille showed in the glue story.

Regardless, the plant and accounting worked well together over the ensuing years paving the way to success. Bruce Ryan says he actually believes good communication among all of Liberty's departments was a key in the company's rise to the top of its industry.

> R. Bruce Ryan
> Accounting Department
> Plant Accountant/Assistant Controller/Controller
> 1982-1992
>
> *"The other company I worked for was much more structured and rigid, and you had many layers of authority you had to go to just about accomplish anything. This can be very annoying and can take much longer to get it approved and implemented in the plant to start seeing the benefits of it."*
>
> *"At Liberty, you had access to the top management immediately if you wanted it. It was kind of like an open-door thing, so you could accomplish things much quicker."*

Today, others in the Accounting Department agree good communication among departments added up to a stronger, more efficient Liberty Glass.

IT Department

Thanks to some very bright minds coupled with education second-to-none, Liberty's IT Department was one of the best in the business. And not just in the glass industry.

Brothers Fulton and Roger Collins were visionaries, but their high-tech dreams would have never become a reality had it not been for men like David Block and David Feiker. Their expertise and hard work enabled the Collins brothers' futuristic vision to become a reality.

David Block came to the IT Department after working his way through Oklahoma State University and summer jobs at Liberty's plant. After graduation, he transferred to the IT Department in the late 1960s, just a few years after it was established, and says he still remembers the department's early days.

David Block
IT Department
IT Department Manager
1967-1994

"Well, they'd really just started the IT department a few years before. It was all cardpunch, so all data was keypunched into data cards and fed into an IBM system. I still remember it was a 360-20 Multi Punch. You fed all the cards into two hoppers, and it calculated everything inside, and then it had hoppers where it could punch out cards for you. Everything was done through an 80-column cardpunch."

"You had the keypunch ladies who took data and transformed it into cards. Payroll would come down as timecards or whatever, and then they would take this data and they would keypunch and produce the cards that would be fed into the machine."

Gary Oyler worked in factory payroll, and he too remembers the challenges in the days before modern computers.

Gary Oyler
Inventory/Payroll
1978-1994

"All manual, adding up the time on the time cards, then check it against the foreman's cards. Any discrepancy you had to go chase down the foreman in the factory. Shift differential was calculated separately."

David Block
IT Department
IT Department Manager
1967-1994

"Then you also had the programmers and system analysts who designed systems, and then you had a computer operator who would take the data cards and run them through to produce reports."

One of those computer operators hired by David Block was his old high school buddy David Feiker, who had been working at Tulsa's First National Bank. The two friends, who had once warmed the bench together for Sapulpa High School's basketball squad, teamed up again, this time to lead Liberty's IT Department.

David Block
IT Department
IT Department Manager
1967-1994

"David [Feiker] was the rock of the IT Department. 100 percent dependable."

David Feiker
IT Department
Programmer/Systems Analyst
1976-1994

"I had worked in the computer department at First National Bank. Mr. Block trained me more than anyone as far as skills go, and he taught me programming and operations. I was the computer operator, and my responsibility was daily operations."

David Feiker went on to become a programmer and systems analyst, and was long considered one of the most valued employees in the department.

As technology advanced, a few years after David Block came to the department he oversaw a complete conversion from IBM to Sperry Univac. It was a data disk-based system, considered to be state-of-the-art at that time.

TO BETTER SERVE YOU...
LIBERTY'S NEW EDP FACILITY

(L to R) Richard J. Kelley, Manager-EDP and Roger B. Collins, Director of Corporate Planning shown at Central Computer.

Liberty Glass has just completed an expansion to the Collins Building which is located in downtown Sapulpa.

The Collins Building houses the Administration offices and the new expansion provides quarters for our growing Data Processing Department.

The new Data Processing Department is one of the finest for its size in the Southwest. The Central Computer provides communications to the various departments.

(L to R) David Fieker, Computer Operator; Bill Fuller, Analyst/Programmer; Richard J. Kelley, EDP Manager; David Block, Analyst/Programmer; Roger B. Collins, Director of Corp. Planning; Dan Edwards, Programmer; and George F. Collins, Jr., President & Chairman of Board.

The Departments of Liberty Glass

Both David Feiker and David Block agree, the IT Department really advanced when Roger Collins, and later, his brother Fulton came to the company in the late '70s and early '80s. Both were well educated and knew that for Liberty to succeed, the company would need to quickly enter the brave new world of technology.

David Block
IT Department
IT Department Manager
1967-1994

"Liberty Glass was state-of-the-art. I can't even imagine another computer department in this part of the country was where we were. Fulton would let you spend anything you wanted as long as you could show him you would make money."

"We were the beta site for Novelle Networking and Microsoft. We got this before anybody else, and we were above state-of-the-art. We were actually so far ahead of state-of-the-art."

"We went heavily into personal computers and networking in the latter part of the '80s."

"We were able to hire a gentleman who was quite eccentric. He was an absolute genius and had two masters by the time he was 21. Claude Sudruff was his name."

"We were doing object-oriented programming. Instead of typing everything, you just clicked a symbol, kind of like Windows."

"We got this before anybody. I don't imagine the companies today even have some of the stuff we had then."

Bill Berry
American Heritage Bank
Chairman

"In many respects Liberty Glass, being not only a leading company within the glass industry, but a leading company in terms of technology enhancements, pushed our bank to make major technology changes. In many cases, we made these changes before they became part of the community banking business. We were trying to keep up with Liberty Glass, and in essence they're part of our success story, and we think we're a part of theirs."

These statements are the consensus regarding the IT Department as it related only to Liberty's administrative functions. The plant also had its own high-tech capabilities, and its own IT group.

David Block
IT Department
IT Department Manager
1967-1994

"The plant had hired an analyst from IBM in Massachusetts, and they brought in their own software. It was like networking software, and they tied all the machines together. The software that was out in the plant was unbelievable. It took measurements and fed them back to the unique mold that had produced the bottle."

"One of the real key aspects of a soda bottle is to have even-wall pressure so they won't break, and it measured the pressure on the bottles. Liberty Glass was the first company in the world to do statistical process control live time on real-time manufacturing."

"The advantage of statistical process control was that it would tell you if something was wrong. If it was trending in the wrong direction, it would tell you before you could make bad bottles…these machines were making 100 bottles a minute."

"There was only one other company that was automated. They were in Ohio, but they couldn't compare to Liberty Glass."

Terry Kelley
Director of Purchasing/
Manager of Engineering Services
1965-2000

"It changed so much. From the time I went to work there until the time I left, the process wasn't even close to being the same. When I went to work there, you could count the bottles on the line. When I left, it looked like a blur. It was just totally different…the equipment was so much better, the automation, the computer operations."

David Feiker
IT Department
Programmer/Systems Analyst
1976-1994

"It was well known throughout the industry that our manufacturing plant was state-of-the-art because of the technology that we had."

It is no surprise that today, as company insiders look back at Liberty Glass and its eventual dominance in the industry, many point to technology and the expertise of the IT Department as key factors.

The Departments of Liberty Glass

Sales Department

The Sales Department at Liberty primarily consisted of two groups. The Inside Sales Group was made up of employees who worked at the office making calls by phone and taking care of the logistics of getting the product delivered correctly and on time. There was also the Outside Sales Division. This group was constantly on the road traveling from customer to customer touting Liberty's glassware. Industry conventions were also a great opportunity for the company's Sales Department to market their products.

Under George Collins Jr., members of the Outside Sales Group were given a new car every year. This did not sit too well with some of those in other departments, but apparently George wanted his personnel to look prosperous when they drove up to a client's office.

Due to his declining health, some say the Sales Department, much like the plant, had become unfocused in George's later years. Just as it happened in the plant when Jim Bolin took over, the Sales Department also underwent major changes when their new leader came to the company. His name was Wills Young, an East Coast man with extensive experience in the glass industry. He was a big man with bold ideas and, like Jim Bolin, Wills brought a whole new way of doing things to Liberty Glass.

Linda Campbell
Sales Department
Receptionist

"We were scared to death. Everything was all so new."

Wills Young
Sales Department
Vice President
1980-1994

"I worked with all the guys, the people in the field and those customers, and I also worked with the inside sales group. So whatever had to be done connected to customers and to our sales people, I did."

"When I got there the total sales department was about 20 people, and that included inside and outside sales people."

"We had too many people for what they were doing, because the market was in the middle of a change. Returnables were no longer big sales. The market had moved over to non-returnables."

Wills Young
Sales Department
Vice President
1980-1994

"We went to a pre-labeled glass container. We were selling glass all over the country. You could afford in those days to even ship returnables to Boston and California. But when we went to non-returnables, pre-labeled, suddenly the distance we could cover shrunk. We didn't need all the people we had, and they weren't working very hard. They were running thru the motions for the most part. Changes had to be made, and I guess that's why they got me in there."

"When I got there they were driving all over the place. They wouldn't let guys fly because they thought it was cheaper to drive. We immediately made that change, and changed some other things that had been going on for years."

ANOTHER *Profitable* YEAR

Wills says Liberty gradually began to do business with customers they had failed to sell for years. Oklahoma City Coca-Cola was their first big breakthrough account, followed by Oklahoma City Pepsi, but this was only the beginning. Liberty next landed three Coca-Cola accounts in the major markets of Houston, Dallas and Fort Worth.

Wills Young
Sales Department
Vice President
1980-1994

"We started selling them and became friends with them and developed relationships. Suddenly the sales started going up. Liberty Glass was doing about $35 million annually when I got there. Fourteen years later, we were doing $100 million with a cheaper product. We were selling more units at a reduced price."

Even though Linda Campbell, Sales Department Receptionist, was at first scared of the changes brought by Wills Young, she soon learned his way of doing things could be exciting. She says the group became much more disciplined and successful under his leadership.

Linda Campbell
Sales Department
Receptionist

"I saw a lot of organized meetings and schedules for the sales staff. They all had different regions, and Alynne Giese and I did the paperwork for all those truckloads they were selling."

"It was all papers then, no computers. And each truckload had a receipt. When I came it was Worrell Dees [Sales Department Manager] and then when Wills came… everybody had a job and everybody got out. They would work for days and days on contracts, and if one word was wrong they would rewrite the contract so the customer would accept it."

Without computers tracking the increased sales, keeping up with all the new orders was no easy task in those days. However, the staff at that time had never known anything differently, so all that paperwork did not seem to be a problem.

Alynne Giese
Sales Department/Quality Control
1960-1988

"Everything was written down in files, including all the tax information. First all the orders would go out every morning and every evening… we had mail runs to the factory from downtown."

"So sometimes trucks would be out there waiting, but the mail hadn't come. The orders hadn't gotten out there yet. Then they changed and finally… I don't' think it was really called a fax machine, but it was something we did on the phone, and we would send out the orders that way."

"And then eventually they got keypunch, and that helped."

Of course Liberty eventually entered the computer age with a world-class IT Department, and without question the efforts of the sales division were greatly enhanced. However, Wills Young says his group's achievements were primarily based on one simple fact.

Wills Young
Sales Department
Vice President
1980-1994

"The only thing we could rely on was our customers' trust in us, that we would do what we said we would do. Once that was established we relied on them and they relied on us, and a feeling of trust was developed."

"We had to sink or swim with our customers, and our ability to maintain a strong ongoing relationship."

"Before I got here our sales group in those days was really not up to the task of building relationships. That was one of the reasons they got me over here... I was over on the East Coast, and the East Coast is highly competitive. Liberty Glass had suddenly run into almost the end of the road with returnables."

"Liberty was switching from 10% returnables to 100% pre-labeled containers. A new effort, a new focus, and suddenly things began to click. That meant tremendous growth year after year."

Of course, growth for Liberty was welcome news to the entire city of Sapulpa. As a result, the community was always eager to help when needed.

Judge Rick Woolery
Judge of District Court
Sapulpa Historical Museum President
Sapulpa Community Leader

"Most of my life, anytime you were asked to do something for Liberty Glass, you did. I remember getting a call in early February one year in the early '90s, and it was from David Beyer. Liberty was trying to get a contract to make beer bottles for a big vendor out of St. Louis. Their marketing director wanted to come down and meet with Liberty, but he also wanted to go quail hunting. I reminded David Beyer that quail season was closing and that the birds were all gone. However, a friend and I called around, and we found someone who had access to a ranch in the Osage. We had a great hunt, and a great time."

Unfortunately, Judge Woolery remembers that Liberty did not get this particular account, but it was the OPPORTUNITY for success that mattered and that's what brought Sales Manager Wills Young all the way to Sapulpa from his native New Jersey. Today Wills remembers when he was offered the job he even had to look on a map to see where Oklahoma was located.

The Departments of Liberty Glass

Linda Campbell
Sales Department/Receptionist

"I think he saw the leadership opportunity not only for him, but for Liberty. We were just going along, and then Wills made the improvements. And the computer came along and we stepped up with the big boys."

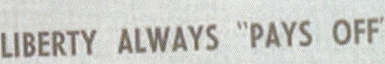

Alynne Giese
Sales Department/Quality Control
1960-1988

"It was refreshing."

Wills Young
Sales Department/Vice President
1980-1994

"We made good quality products, and we always did what we said we were going to do."

The Departments of Liberty Glass

Chapter Eight

The Strike of 1983

No event in the history of Liberty Glass impacted the company like the Strike of 1983. For over 70 years the plant had operated as a place of relative peace, but all that changed in the spring of 1983.

Management, led by Fulton Collins, and the Union couldn't come to an agreement on a management rights clause in the plant's union contract, and the workers went on strike April 1. Approximately 350 members of the Glass, Pottery and Plastic Allied Workers Locals 185 and 128 were involved.

Surprisingly, the dispute was not prompted by wages, but by a disagreement over the company's benefits package. According to union officials, the benefits being disputed involved insurance, vacation and retirement. At the time, Liberty representatives claimed the company simply wanted to "exercise the right to utilize employees' time and skills where they are needed, without restrictions".

Jim Bolin
Plant Manager/President
1977-1994

"It was actually a benefit for retirees. That was one of Fulton's adamant stands. He said, 'We're one company, we can't do what someone else [larger organizations] can do'."

"The only thing the International Union representative wanted was a dime an hour for every retiree that ever retired, which is a ton of money. This was not a benefit for any one worker working. Companies are responsible to pay that retirement anyhow, but you can't keep adding to it."

Glen F. Nix
Supervisor Maintenance/
Batch and Furnace
1953-1994

"When they went on strike, I had just moved into the company. I had a bunch of friends who went on strike, and that bothered me a lot because I was in the company. But I had to work and go on... you've just got to take it and go with it."

Johnny L. Brison
Plant Maintenance/
Plant Maintenance Supervisor
1959-1999

"I knew they were going on strike. I worked in a high enough office with Jim Bolin, and I knew the people weren't coming back. I was walking them to the gate, and I begged them to come back. I knew they couldn't come back after they walked out, because the company wasn't going to hire them back."

"When you begged them not to go out there and they go anyway you can't help them. They were good people."

Roger Collins
Son of George Collins Jr.
Management
1977-1981

"It was not Fulton's intent to replace the Union. He just did not think the company could remain competitive if he did not hold firm in the negotiations. What he did not know when the strike began was that American Airlines was to have a major layoff that would enable Liberty to hire skilled workers to replace those on strike. In the end that is what enabled Liberty to become non-union. It was not envisioned at the beginning of the strike. It was simply about company survival. He was certainly not interested in putting our long time employees out of work."

The Strike of 1983

Susie Collins
Wife of Fulton Collins

> "Fulton said he would cross the picket line, and probably live at the plant and he did for a while. It was violent. Lives were threatened. His was threatened. I never knew if, when he left for work, he'd come home alive at the end of the day."

> "I will never forget it…When the strike started Fulton sent me and our daughters to live with his mother in Florida. We did not see him for three weeks. When we eventually returned to Tulsa, we had two armed guards around the clock. We had guards on our property until our last daughter left for college 18 years later."

Susie also recalls that the Collins' youngest daughter was nicknamed "the strike baby" because she was born eight days before the strike started.

As one would expect, the strike garnered statewide media attention, as seen in these articles, originally published by the Daily Oklahoman in Oklahoma City.

STRIKING GLASSWORKES in Sapulpa Saturday revieved a show of support from other state unions in the form of food and cash donations. Gathering at strike headquarters were: (l-r) Pete Dodson, union executive officer; Lavoid Meek, union president from Ada; Louis Hood, Sapulpa union president; John Sanders, a state AFL vice president; Ross Williams, state AFL-CIO secretary treasurer; Wayne Bradley, union president from and Wayne Buckley, a Sapulpa union president. (photo by Curt Reed)

THE OKLAHOMAN

Sapulpa Union Workers Anxious for End to Glass Firm Strike

Margaret Dornaus/ Published: May 15, 1983.   Republished with permission of The Oklahoman

In 1913, George F. Collins Sr. founded Liberty Glass Co. to manufacture glass bottles that are now shipped to soft drink plants throughout the world and in most parts of the United States.

Today, Liberty Glass is Sapulpa's largest industrial plant. It has, during its three generations of operation, employed a sizable portion of the residents of this small northeastern Oklahoma town, many of whom have never held jobs outside the factory gates.

But after nearly 70 years of smooth operation as a union plant and three generations of Collins family management, Liberty Glass has replaced its regular work force with non-union employees.

The 474 members of locals 128 and 185 of the Glass, Pottery and Plastic Allied Workers Union have been on strike since April 1 over a "management rights" clause that the founder's grandson and company president, Fulton Collins, wants included in the laborers' contract.

Negotiations are at an impasse.

The company's attorney, William Toney of Tulsa, says management simply wants to exercise the right to "utilize employees' time and skills where they are needed without restrictions."

That means the company can take a worker off his assigned job and put him on any other job in the factory for any period of time. Pay rate for reclassification is conspicuously absent from the contract language.

Toney says the workers' pay rate would not change, but they don't believe it.

"It's the wording that's wrong," said Keith Cox one day last week as he began his four-hour shift walking the picket line in front of one of Liberty's gates.

Cox, who has worked for the plant for the past 10 years, said such a clause would jeopardize his job security. He is afraid the company would then be able to transfer him from his job in the "hot-end," or forming area of the plant, to a lesser-skilled and lower-paying position.

"I've worked six years to classify myself," Cox said.

Wayne Buckley, president of the production and maintenance workers Local 185, has worked for Liberty Glass for 27 years. Before he went out on strike six weeks ago, he was earning $11.24 an hour. Today, the union workers are drawing $50 a week from a strike fund for walking four hours a day in front of the company's gates.

Money is not the issue, said Buckley; union members didn't even ask for a raise.

"There were no raises in the contract," he said. "Over a three-year period, we've been raised a $1.05 an hour and we've never fought it." The issue, he said, has to do with management rights and seniority.

"The department I work in gets the highest pay," hot-end worker Allen Sutton said.

Sutton has worked for Liberty Glass for 17 years. It is the first and only job he has ever had except for the two years he served with the armed forces during the Vietnam War.

"The management rights clause would have done away with seniority," said Sutton. "They want to stick us in another department and they didn't say they would pay us at the same rate. They could have me cleaning the bathrooms."

Sutton and his wife, Sandy, have two children. Mrs. Sutton works as an aide at a local nursing home. She said her income will pay for the family's living expenses during the time her husband remains on strike.

"We may lose some luxuries, but we'll eat and survive," she said.

A luxury in the Sutton household is a second car. "There's a lot of them out there that don't have any money," she said.

Mrs. Sutton expressed sympathy for those who have family members requiring medical attention. She explained that the strikers have to pay the company a $205-a-month premium in order to continue receiving insurance coverage.

We're organizing a garage sale to raise money for the people who are the neediest and local people and merchants have donated food to try to keep all heads above water," she said.

Recently, Mrs. Sutton organized a march with about 150 of the striking workers' friends and relatives protesting outside the Liberty Glass plant.

"The purpose of the march was to get the public to communicate with Mr. Collins and encourage him to meet with union officials and go back to the bargaining table," Mrs. Sutton said.

Repeated attempts by a reporter to contact Collins by telephone were unsuccessful.

Mrs. Sutton plans to stage a second march that she hopes will attract an even larger number of protesters later this month.

"There have been no union employees participating in our march," she added quickly, explaining that the company was eager to find the union in violation of a May 4 injunction that forbids mass picketing at Liberty Glass.

The union workers have observed that injunction. Only six workers picket at any one time at the plant with two marchers positioned at each entrance to the plant.

Uniformed guards stand watch over the 24-hour demonstration and escort company officials to and from work each day.

Union officials said the guards, like many of the replacement workers, were brought in from other states.

"Some of the guards are mouthy," Cox said. "They tried to provoke us, but we've got to keep it peaceful." The strike has, for the most part, been peaceful.

Assistant police chief Johnny Moore said the strike has been "pretty quiet." But that was before a fire-bombing incident reported early Wednesday.

Workers place picket at Liberty Glass

At 3 a.m., neighbors reported a car afire at the home of Daniel Diaz, a replacement worker in the Liberty Glass plant. Police reports said a quart beer bottle filled with a flammable substance had been tossed into the car while Diaz was at work. Moore said the car was gutted.

Before that time, only two other incidents of violence had been linked to the strike. During the first week of labor dispute, a tire was slashed on a truck that was hauling glassware.

On April 29, security guards reported that four pop bottles containing what was believed to be a flammable substance were tossed into a fenced parking lot across from the plant. One of the bottles hit a parked vehicle, damaging the front windshield.

Only one of the makeshift Molotov cocktails exploded. No one was injured and no arrests were made.

Buckley says he knows nothing about either of the fire-bombing incidents. He suspects that the April 29 episode might have been planned to give the strikers bad publicity.

"We don't know anything about it," he said. "None of us did it."

Most of the workers walking the picket line have worked for Liberty Glass for 10 to 35 years. All are anxious for a settlement so they can return to work.

"We're going to try to win this legally," said Sutton. "Either they go broke or I do. If that's what it takes, that's what it takes."

Only six weeks have elapsed since the strike began. Company attorney and spokesman Toney last week called the strike "old news."

"It's like saying Elizabeth Taylor got a divorce," he said. But the people who have set up strike headquarters in Sally's Grill, a tiny diner next to the foreman's parking lot at Liberty Glass, have their eyes on the outcome of the strike 24 hours a day. They are hoping their strike does not become "as old" as the one held at the Bartlett-Collins plant down the road.

That strike lasted eight years before new management agreed last week to accept a contract establishing a union shop at the plant.

The Strike of 1983

Union Concerned About Violence in Liberty Glass Strike

Margaret Dornaus/ Published: June 3, 1983. Republished with permission of The Oklahoman

Officials of the Glass, Pottery and Plastic Allied Workers Union held a press conference Thursday to discuss recent violence in a two-month-long strike at the Liberty Glass Co. plant in Sapulpa.

More than 350 members of locals 128 and 185 of GPPAW have been on strike at the plant since April 1 when the contract offered by company president Fulton Collins was rejected because of a controversial "management rights" clause. Workers think management's demands could jeopardize their job security and classifications.

Since then, several incidents of violence have been linked to the strike. On May 11, a car was firebombed at the residence of Daniel Diaz, a replacement worker at the plant. Last week, police reported that the windows of a guard house at the plant had been shot out with a pellet gun.

Union representatives claim no knowledge or responsibility for any of the incidents. They do, however, fear that additional violence may occur if the guards provided by Security Investigation Ltd. of Tulsa decide to arm themselves.

GPPAW International official Wallace "Pete" Dodson of Broken Arrow claims the arming of security guards in a strike situation may be against Oklahoma law.

"We want no violence," Dodson said, adding that armed guards might "precipitate violence."

"This is no longer a labor dispute," Dodson continued. "This is a vendetta. There may be a possibility of people carrying guns out there while we're carrying picket signs. This is a volatile, highly emotional, very sensitive environment we're talking about."

$5,000 REWARD

Liberty Glass Company is offering a reward for information leading to the arrest and felony conviction of the person or persons who are responsible for the commission of any of the following crimes or unlawful acts against current employees of Liberty Glass Company and their families:

The firebombing of an automobile around 3:15 AM on Wednesday, May 11, 1983.

The shooting of a residence around 12:05 AM on Friday, May 13, 1983.

The burning of a residence around 5:00 AM on about Tuesday, June 21, 1983.

Liberty Glass Talks Resume
Published: September 28, 1983. Republished with permission of The Oklahoman

SAPULPA Striking glass workers and representatives of Liberty Glass Co. here have reopened talks for the first time in about five months, an attorney for the firm said Tuesday.

Representatives of the company and the Glass, Pottery, Plastics and Allied Workers union met Monday, and planned a second meeting for next month, said the attorney, Bill Toney of Tulsa. In the meantime, union officials will consider offers by the company, he said.

No date has been announced for the second meeting.

Monday's meeting was the first meeting since April, when the 300 members went on strike, Toney said.

"There was some change of positions, but nothing in terms of reaching an agreement," Toney said of Monday's discussions.

However, he said, "I'm glad they're meeting, that's better than hitting people with ball bats."

Several months ago, five pickets allegedly were involved in a fracas outside the plant that hospitalized two security guards. A Creek County court hearing for some of the accused is set for today.

The strike impacted those involved in a variety of ways. For Liberty's non-union employees, it meant filling in at the plant for the striking union members.

Accountants, secretaries, IT and sales personnel all found themselves doing jobs they'd never been trained to do.

Wills Young
Sales Department
Vice President
1980-1994

"We survived, but it was a tough time. Everybody in the company was assigned responsibilities at the factory, because we lost all factory people."

"I was the only sales guy taking care of all of these customers… because everyone else was at the plant."

David Block
IT Department/IT Department Manager
1967-1994

"It was kind of like an armed camp for a while. We were 12 on and 12 off. I worked from 7 in the morning to 7 at night."

"We still had to run the payroll, and we still had to do some other functions."

Gary Oyler
Inventory/Payroll
1978-1996

"Somebody else did the payroll, and they put me out running the palletizer that hadn't quite gotten installed. That was an interesting job and I got to work out in the factory for a few days, until they needed me to get back in and start doing payroll again."

Michael K. Wille
Accounting Department
1974-1989

"We all had our positions assigned for when the strike came. I remember I was going to be a floor boy at the end of this row where the boxes of bottles came off and we would palletize them. I realized after two days of this that they needed someone to do accounting during the production, and I found myself a new job."

Johnny L. Brison
Plant Maintenance/
Plant Maintenance Supervisor
1959-1999

"It was tough on the company personnel."

"We could make the bottles, but we couldn't get them off the floor because we didn't have the automated machines. All those guys from downtown, guys like David Beyer and Bruce Ryan, worked their guts out trying to keep it alive. We finally survived."

For the striking union workers, it was a very different concern. They were suddenly worried over the loss of a steady paycheck, but for all those involved, no concern was greater than the very real threat of violence.

By August of 1983, as the strike entered into its fifth month, the weather grew hotter, as did the tempers on both sides of the conflict. An August 19th article in the Sapulpa Herald described "armed security guards forming a ring around the plant". This came after violence erupted the night before, causing injury to five people, including a number of the guards. Four former employees were initially arrested and charged with assault with a deadly and dangerous weapon. Authorities continued to search for two more suspects.

There was seemingly no end to the bitter conflict. Throughout the year and into the next, reports of arson, rioting, gunplay, vandalism and an endless array of accusations seemed to be the norm. Today, Susie Collins remembers how stressful the strike was for everyone involved.

UNION SUPPORTERS Friday staged a second protest march in an attempt to convince Liberty Glass Co. President Fulton Collins to intervene in the seven-week-old labor dispute between his company and two Glass, Pottery, Plastics and Allied Workers Union locals. The marchers, which began walking about 4:30 p.m., held the protest walk in front of the glass plant and south along Mission Avenue. (Herald photo)

Susie Collins
Wife of Fulton Collins

"We brought in a swat team from Kentucky that deals with coal mine strikes. I remember how horrible people were to the employees that crossed the picket lines. Shots were fired into their homes, cattle run off, fences torn down. It was complicated, because many employees were related to one another as spouses, siblings or relatives."

Sapulpa Daily HERALD — Thursday, June 2, 1983

Liberty security guards may arm selves
Violence brings warning to union, Creek County sheriff

The Strike of 1983

Striking union members even went so far as to seek a restraining order against Liberty Glass and Security and Investigations Ltd in an effort to keep the security guards and other workers from carrying any firearms. Judge Donald Thompson granted their request on August 23, and his ruling prohibited guards from openly carrying guns at the plant.

To boost plant protection, Thompson ordered Sapulpa police officers and Creek County sheriff deputies to patrol the plant 30 minutes before and after each shift change.

As the strike wore on throughout 1983 and into 1984, the continuing stress became almost unbearable for Fulton Collins and his young family.

Susie Collins
Wife of Fulton Collins

"Fulton said, 'I don't think I can keep it running for a week. We've got to settle the strike'. The strike lasted 21 months, almost two solid years."

The end finally came in early 1985. The Sapulpa Herald made the announcement with these words. "After 21 months of aggravation, violence, no pay and no benefits, the [Liberty Glass] strike finally ended."

Liberty Glass replacement workers voted the Union out as the National Labor Relations Board had made the decision not to count the votes of Liberty's striking workers.

After the votes were counted, union representatives, bitter with disappointment, left without meeting with members of the press who had gathered.

It was a victory for the Collins family, but a somewhat bittersweet one, as the strike had taken its toll. It was a dark and dangerous time in the history of Liberty Glass, and for everyone involved, the Strike of 1983 remains a painful memory today.

For those who had weathered the storm together, it wasn't easy picking up the pieces after the strike. The company had taken a huge financial hit, but once the clouds cleared, everyone agreed that Liberty started to become a much better place to work. Gradually, employees developed a newfound passion and a greater sense of pride.

David Beyer
Accounting Department
Chief Financial Officer
1972-1994

"We went from (us versus them) in the strike; and really it had been that way for a long time, to (we)."

Now united, Liberty looked to its future and hoped for a brighter tomorrow. Little did they know the turnaround would be better than anyone dared to dream.

Jim Bolin
Plant Manager/President
1977-1994

"It became a real fun place to work. It really did."

The Strike of 1983

Chapter Nine

The Turnaround

After the strike, Liberty identified two primary goals. One was to quickly move to the leading edge of technology, and the second called for the company to become the low-cost and best quality producer of soft drink bottles within Liberty's service area. This area was defined as east to Chicago, north to Minneapolis-St. Paul, west to Denver and south to Dallas. The area represented about 14% of the U.S. market and was determined by Liberty's freight rates compared to its competitors. This area identified locations where Liberty had either the same freight cost or a cost advantage

David Beyer
Accounting Department
Chief Financial Officer
1972-1994

"Fulton Collins and Jim Bolin developed a business plan that capitalized on their individual personal strengths. Fulton understood the principles of how a business should operate and succeed. These principles applied to all businesses. In the beginning he knew very little about producing glass bottles, but Jim Bolin knew how to produce glass bottles and had significant container glass industry experience. Together Fulton and Jim were quite a team."

Jim Bolin
Plant Manager/President
1977-1994

"At my request, David Beyer had previously developed the daily manufacturing cost reporting system, which became the platform for all of the future planning and was the financial platform for the business plan. Already having this system in place allowed Fulton to grasp the glass industry very quickly, and was instrumental in our success."

From that point forward, Liberty developed a fluid strategy designed to adapt to the demands of an ever-changing marketplace. The most important examples of this were the major capital expenditures that would give the company a competitive advantage in its market area, as well as any capital expenditures that would be paid back in one year.

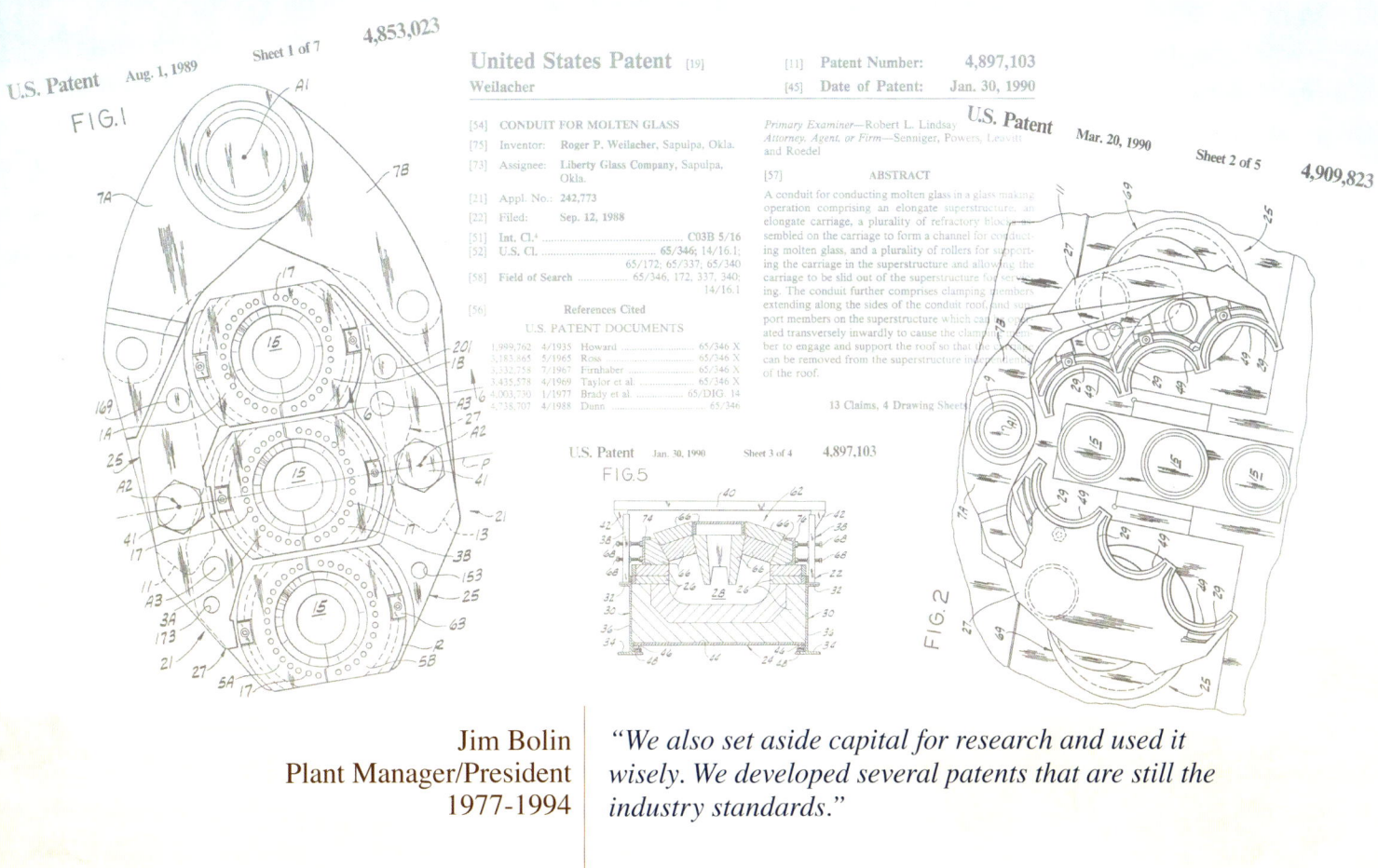

Jim Bolin
Plant Manager/President
1977-1994

"We also set aside capital for research and used it wisely. We developed several patents that are still the industry standards."

This aggressive position allowed Liberty not only to prosper, but to expand its service area to Atlanta, Georgia, the U.S. headquarters of Coca-Cola.

Liberty's Sales Department also did its share in ensuring the strategy's success, by selling the annual increase in plant capacity. To reduce its unit costs, Liberty designed high production triple gob bottle machines that led the industry in production performance, yielding significantly lower unit costs than plastic and glass competitors.

The increased production performance also resulted in downstream line upgrades, such as automated stackers, more efficient inspection equipment and an in-house production monitoring system. These glass production improvements were accomplished by company personnel and resulted in the Liberty plant becoming one of the best in the world. By the mid-1980s, Liberty had doubled its market share to 90% of the soft drink sales in its service area. This one-plant company represented 2% of total container (beer and soft drink) sales in the United States.

David Beyer
Accounting Department
Chief Financial Officer
1972-1994

"Early on our strategy recognized that plastic bottles were a greater threat to us than our competitors in the glass industry. This was due to lower unit manufacturing costs in plastics."

Jim Bolin
Plant Manager/President
1977-1994

"Today, the plastic bottle is the soft drink container of choice. In the larger size 64 ounce soda container, the soda companies began to market the safety of plastic vs. glass. The danger of mothers driving home from the supermarket with a two liter plastic bottle (implied unbreakable without saying it), rolling around in the back of a SUV, was their large national roll out on prime time TV."

"Liberty, however, was able to continue to compete with plastic on cost."

David Beyer
Accounting Department
Chief Financial Officer
1972-1994

"Fulton Collins wanted to be better and he wanted everyone around him to be better. As far as we were concerned, we were the best glass company in the world, and it was Fulton's leadership that got us there."

"We had visitors from all over the world. Everyone wanted to see what we were doing."

Susie Collins
Wife of Fulton Collins

"It was amazing what Fulton and Jim Bolin did in a down economy in the glass industry, and kept it going…they created one of the most modern plants in the country."

David Beyer
Accounting Department
Chief Financial Officer
1972-1994

"Both Fulton and Jim understood that they would not be successful without a talented and aggressive workforce that would take ownership of the business plan."

With this in mind, Fulton Collins developed new policies that emphasized a cooperative approach in almost every facet of the business.

Jim Bolin
Plant Manager/President
1977-1994

"We set up a committee for the hourly people whenever we had a discipline problem. We had two salaried people and two hourly, and we would present our problem and there was a vote across the board. And they were tougher than any salaried group."

David Beyer
Accounting Department
Chief Financial Officer
1972-1994

"That was a big positive for our company. Our employees definitely had a voice. All that aggravation going back and forth went away, and it was always "we". Several times a year we had employee meetings."

"We paid x cents or a percent above the average wage in the area. We wanted to be in the upper range, not in the lower. We did surveys every year to make sure our jobs were above the average pay."

"It was a team, not just a management team, but a company team."

Fulton Collins and his team of Liberty employees staged one of the most dramatic turnarounds in the history of the glass industry. The outcome was far greater than any of them ever imagined, but the group also knew that the glass industry, as it existed, would not last forever. As plastics continued to evolve down to the smaller sizes, it became clear that Liberty needed to quickly diversify into the beer business.

Jim Bolin
Plant Manager/President
1977-1994

"We could see the end wasn't far away in this product mix. We began to pursue the beer market, starting with Budweiser. My first meeting with Budweiser was a suppliers' meeting with all major glass suppliers present. The industry knew of our manufacturing advantages, and this eventually led to the sale of Liberty Glass. I believe this was our first serious contact with American National Can, the parent company of Foster Forbes that would eventually buy Liberty Glass."

The Turnaround

Chapter Ten

Fulton's Finest Hour

After surviving the strike and successfully establishing Liberty as a major player in the glass industry, Fulton Collins was exhausted both physically and mentally. Having achieved his goals for the company, Fulton began to consider selling Liberty sometime in the early nineties. By 1994 he knew he was ready, although for him selling was a complicated decision.

Roger Collins
Brother of Fulton Collins

"It was very emotional for Fulton to sell Liberty Glass because it had been in the family forever."

David Beyer
Accounting Department
Chief Financial Officer
1972-1994

Red Carpet is out for Foster Forbes

Just what is Foster Forbes Glass Co., and why did they buy Liberty Glass?

In short, Foster Forbes, of Marion, Ind., is a division of American National Can, a multinational company with sales of more than $4 billion yearly. ANC, in turn, is a subsidiary of Pechiney International, S.A., a Paris-based, publicly traded company and a member of the group companies of Pechiney, S.A.

ANC produces a wide variety of metal, glass and plastic packaging products for the beverage, food and personal care markets.

Jean-Louis Vinciguerra is Pechiney's chairman and chief executive officer. Jack Turner is the ANC president and CEO, North America.

The president of Foster Forbes is

became into being as the result of natural gas deposits discovered in Indiana in the late 1800s.

The first corporate charter was issued to Upland Flint Bottle Co. in 1911 in Upland, Ind., and the name was changed to Foster Forbes a few years later. The company moved from Upland to Marion in 1923 and in 1930, acquired a neighboring company.

In 1950, an entirely new factory was built at the current Marion location. In 1966, a new and modern plant became operational in Burlington, Wis.

The biggest change in company operations came about in 1970, when National Can Corp. of Chicago acquired Foster Forbes and it became the glass division of a major corporation. With that acquisition, National also bought another glass plant at Oil

"All I really know is that I think it would be fair to say that there was speculation, and I've confirmed this with a couple of people, that more than likely Fulton had a three or four year plan to sell the company. That was his goal. There were things the company could do, and he was positioning us."

"I may have been the first one on the staff to know about it. I met with Fulton at an airport hangar at Tulsa International Airport. We met with the CFO of American Can. American Can owned Foster Forbes. The deal, the sale, was negotiated on the back of an envelope in about 30 minutes. The basic structure of the deal was hammered out in an airport hangar in less than an hour."

Liberty was sold to Foster Forbes in 1994. Some employees stayed on with the new group, but today most remember things were never the same after Liberty. Of course that's often the case, as it's never easy to replace a loyal, locally owned company with a group from out of town.

Liberty Glass sold to ANC

By DON DIEHL
Herald Staff Writer

It's official.

Liberty Glass Company, a Sapulpa based company since 1912, has been sold to American National Can Company, a division of Foster-Forbes headquartered in Marion, Ind.

Liberty and ANC announced this morning that a "definite agreement" had been reached between the two

headquartered in France. Foster-Forbes corporate offices are in Chicago.

Rumors of the pending sale had been circulating for more than a month. The topic came up at Monday night's meeting of the Sapulpa Board of City Commissioners in an apparently un-related issue of the donation of a company parking lot.

technological advances and progress of Liberty," Thompson said. "It is one of the best, if not the best, glass container producers in the country."

The amount of the sale and other details of the agreement were not disclosed.

Liberty is one of the top 10 taxpayers in Creek County, paying more than $300,000 in taxes last year.

Last year, it reported net sales of $80 million.

ANC's glass-making operations, which markets under the Foster-Forbes name, showed sales of $577 million in 1993.

Thompson said that ANC would continue operating the plant in the same "high quality way" it has been operated.

Thompson said that the sale of

manufacturers — provides a secure future for the company, its employees and standing in the community.

Thompson said that ANC had approached Liberty as early as 1987 about a possible sale or consolidation. Talks on the current agreement began in June of last year.

Thompson said that he had been to Sapulpa four or five times during the

For Fulton Collins, the sale came as a relief, and he then turned to focus on his family and the community he loved. Fulton and his wife Susie enjoyed exercising together, as both were committed to a life of fitness. They also loved to travel, and combined these two interests with bicycling trips all over the world.

Susie Collins
Wife of Fulton Collins

"He never thought of himself as an athlete, but he loved exercise and he became very fit."

Throughout his life, Fulton had always been a devoted father, but now that he no longer had an all-consuming career he gave even greater attention to his children. Susie says when their daughters were in high school and college, Fulton bought their same textbooks, and would follow along in their studies.

In spite of his great success in business and as a family man, most agree Fulton Collins will be remembered by most for his service and generosity to the Tulsa Community.

He worked with the Children's Medical Center and Hillcrest Healthcare System, Tulsa Chamber of Commerce, Tulsa Philharmonic, Tulsa and Westside YMCA, Tulsa Chapter of the American Red Cross, Young Presidents' Organization, World Presidents' Organization and the Sapulpa Chamber of Commerce.

Fulton's greatest commitment was to education. The foundation of his belief was in a life of learning, which was clearly defined by his countless contributions in terms of both time and money to the University of Tulsa. Family members say that while the Collins' Foundations have long supported TU, Fulton heavily invested his personal funds from the sale of Liberty into the school.

Fulton's bio on TU's website states, "[Fulton's] ability to inspire was matched only by his desire to see others thrive, as evidenced by a legacy of enhancements he spearheaded at The University of Tulsa."

| Steadman Upham
University of Tulsa President | *"His whole being was organized around how to make things better, how to change them for the better."*

"One of the things I truly loved about Fulton was his creative impatience. He was the kind of person who loved change." |

Under his leadership as Chairman of the Board of Trustees, TU doubled its endowment, doubled the value of its land and buildings, doubled its research funding and more than doubled undergraduate admissions.

On May 10, 2008, the University of Tulsa surprised Fulton by awarding him the first honorary degree from the newly renamed Collins College of Business. During his involvement with TU, Fulton considered many of the students there his personal friends, and they came to know him as a role model both in business and in life.

Eric
Former TU Association President

"He was never satisfied until he could tell that every single student was happy and was really engaged on campus."

Robert Lorton Jr.
Brother of Fulton Collins

"The University of Tulsa, to a very great degree, is a reflection of Fulton's vision and leadership."

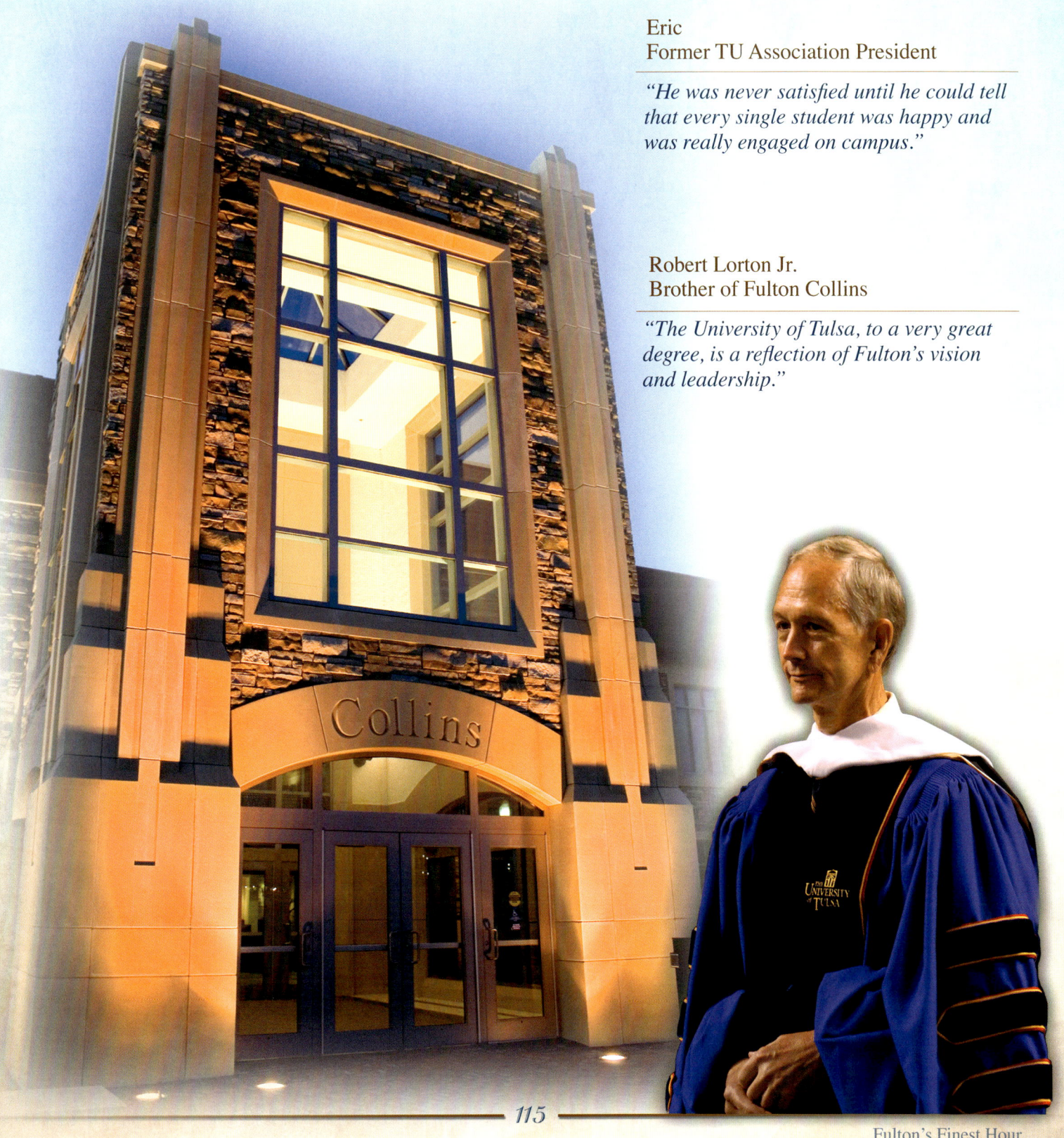

Fulton's Finest Hour

Like so many others in the community, Roger Collins is proud of what his brother accomplished in life, and even though the siblings' business partnership ended years earlier, Roger says the two continued to enjoy spending time together.

As history tells us, sometimes the bond between brothers can be complicated, as it was with the Collins' siblings. All that changed when Fulton was diagnosed with a very rare and fast-acting form of cancer.

Like most families faced with a crisis, it was now "us against the world." During Fulton's treatment it was determined that he needed a bone marrow transplant, and the best match was Roger. Suddenly two brothers who were once conflicted in business now reconnected to battle cancer.

Roger Collins
Brother of Fulton Collins

"I was a bone marrow donor for him because I was the best match…he was never healthy enough to accept it. I think it floored him that I was a bone marrow donor for him. I don't think he had any idea that I would do that."

"I think it helped us bond more, and repair some of the wounds that had been there frankly, and some of the tears. And that was good."

Sadly, Fulton Collins lost his battle with cancer and passed away in 2008 at age 65. For Susie and the rest of the family, it was not easy moving forward after his death. Fulton's spirit and vitality had played a major role in everyone's lives.

Susie Collins
Wife of Fulton Collins

"I miss his companionship. We were absolutely best friends. He used to say, 'do you realize how lucky we are?' We had a great marriage."

"He was a really hard worker. I think he appreciated everything he ever had in life, and he just took that and built on it. I consider him a self-made man."

Suzanne Collins Yonkers
Daughter of Fulton Collins

"I miss talking to him, asking his advice and seeing his smile. I could tell him everything (and did). There isn't a day that goes by that I don't think about him."

Fulton Collins IV
Son of Fulton Collins

"In general I miss him. That's the simplest way of putting it. It's more about his presence. I miss having that person to ask questions. I miss his advice. In overall terms, he's just not there. Sometimes I'll be driving in the car and I'll think, 'Oh I should ask Dad about that' and then I remember I can't."

Chrissy Collins Mantzuranis
Daughter of Fulton Collins

"It is hard to pin what I miss most about dad since I miss all of him. I guess what I wish I had him around for the most these days is his honesty and objective opinion. I am always asking myself when I am stuck in a bad situation or don't know if I am making a good decision 'what would dad do?' or 'how would dad handle this?' He was always so open minded I thought."

Carolyn Collins
Daughter of Fulton Collins

"I miss his energy. He has a way of being here even when he is not. But I still miss him very much."

Robert Lorton Jr.
Brother of Fulton Collins

"What do I miss? Everything… his humor, his insightfulness, his determination, and he was just fun to be around."

Roger Collins
Brother of Fulton Collins

"I miss my brother. I respected him and he respected me as long as we weren't in the same business together." (laugh)

Beverley Collins Ward
Sister of Fulton Collins

"The true answer in one word is [I miss] everything. But I will answer your question by saying his wit, his sense of humor and mainly just being around him."

Unfortunately, Fulton died before all of his projects at the University of Tulsa were completed; however Susie says he was able to make one final visit to campus. After a flight from Houston where Fulton had been receiving treatment at M.D. Anderson Hospital, an ambulance picked the couple up at the Tulsa Airport. Susie told the driver they would need to make a side-trip before going home. She wanted to take Fulton by the TU campus to show him all that had been accomplished while he was away. Because the cancer was causing his eye sight to fail, Susie carefully described the many improvements he had helped to create. Although he could not see every detail, one thing was undoubtedly clear to Fulton Collins: his dream for the University of Tulsa had been fulfilled.

Fulton himself summed up his service to the school by stating it was "the best thing I've ever done." Many would agree, TU was Fulton Collins' finest hour, and was in part made possible by Liberty Glass.

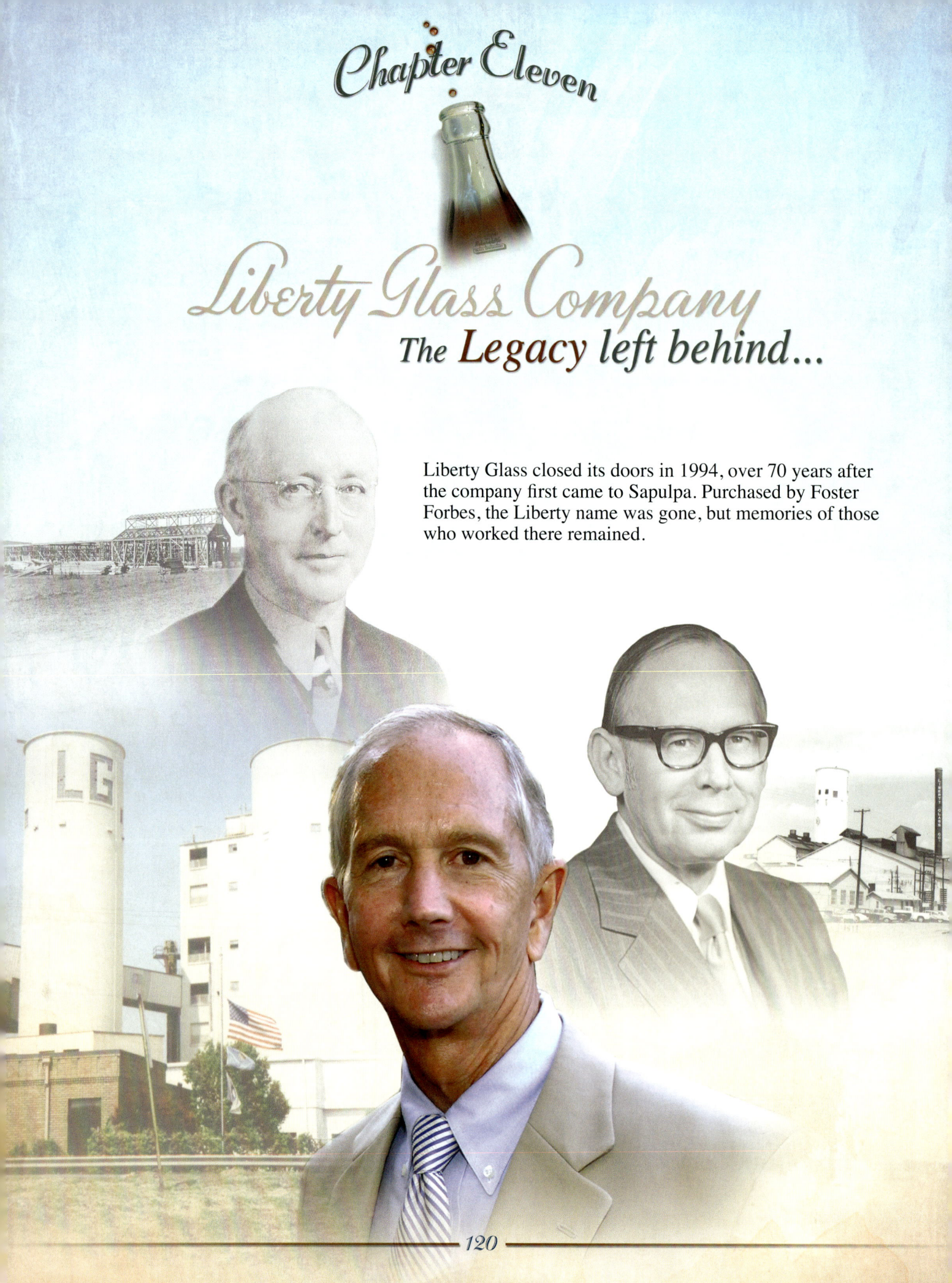

Chapter Eleven

Liberty Glass Company
The Legacy left behind...

Liberty Glass closed its doors in 1994, over 70 years after the company first came to Sapulpa. Purchased by Foster Forbes, the Liberty name was gone, but memories of those who worked there remained.

Over the years, much had changed...yet much stayed the same. New technology came in and old ways walked out the door, and even though Liberty employees tended to stay on for years and sometimes even decades, time brought change to the names and faces at the company. However, the things that stayed the same were this: The people of Liberty had always worked hard, and were always willing to do an honest day's work for an honest day's pay.

After the company closed some employees stayed on with the new group, but today most remember things were never the same after Liberty. Of course that is often the case, as it's never easy to replace a loyal, locally-owned company with a group from out of town.

For those who walked out the door for the last time in 1994, none left empty-handed. They took their experiences, the hardships and heartaches, camaraderie and close friendships they'd come to know. There were hugs and tears and promises to stay in touch. Without question, emotions ruled the day.

David Feiker
IT Department
Programmer/Systems Analyst
1976-1994

"I felt lost. I had a difficult childhood, and I came to Liberty looking for a family, and now that family wouldn't be there. I thought I would be there for the rest of my career. I can still remember I was scared and afraid of the unknown. I had a son ready for college...how was I going to pay for that? We knew a big company like Foster Forbes would have their own IT people, and we would be replaced. Worst of all, I felt like I'd lost my family."

David Feiker was not alone in his feelings. It always was the people that made Liberty special. People who worked hard and tried to do things the right way, but they were also human, and not everything worked perfectly.

The Legacy Left Behind...

Liberty was complicated and conflicted at times. So much could go wrong, even when everyone was trying to do right. There was a never-ending battle to cover all the bases, but not all decisions turned out to be the best ones.

Safety was a constant concern, although no matter what precautions were taken, accidents, sometimes very serious ones, still happened. But the people say they never stopped trying, and they never gave in to failure.

Much like a family always striving to find its way, the men and women of Liberty labored each day trying to do the job for which they had been hired. Sometimes there was a feeling of us against them, management against the workers, but most agreed all that changed after the strike. A new theme took hold at the plant; it was, "Us against the outside world."

Today the imposing batch towers, built during the Liberty era, still loom over the Sapulpa skyline, a symbol to those who worked there. Even though the company has been sold several times since Liberty closed its doors, most say the plant will always mean Liberty Glass to them. There are some things you just can't sell.

Gary Oyler
Inventory/Payroll
1978-1996

"Everybody will always call it Liberty Glass, even though they covered over the LG on the tower and everything, you look up there you still can see that LG. Lots of good times there."

Pete Egan
Sapulpa Community Leader
Author of the book,
"SAPULPA, OK - THE GREATEST CITY IN THE KNOWN WORLD"

"People may not know the name of the plant right now, but they know where Liberty Glass is. At one time we had four glass plants in this town, but Liberty was the first glass plant we had, and it's the only surviving one. I think that speaks volumes for the Collins family to keep it going, and up with technology, and all of those kinds of things."

It has now been 20 years since Liberty was sold, and since that time, many employees have passed on, while others have moved on, each life taking its own twists and turns.

Thanks to the people who made it a success and the generous gifts of the Collins family, the memory of Liberty lives today. Some say the spirit of the company may never die, and nowhere is that more evident than in Sapulpa, the town the company called home for over 76 years.

Philanthropy had always been important to the Collins family going all the way back to George Collins Sr., when he and his wife Jennie started their charitable foundation. The family knew they were fortunate, and wanted to make sure others benefitted from their success. From one generation to the next, the descendants of George Sr. continued down his philanthropic path.

Roger Collins
Son of George Collins Jr.
Management
1977-1981

"My father set up two foundations that were specifically targeted toward, and still are targeted toward, educational gifts and Sapulpa gifts, and so we used that money over the years to give back to the community. And the community gave a lot to us. The community really gave us everything we had. The company is only as good as its people, and the people really allowed us to be here today. I hope people will remember that we were a company that cared about its people."

Ted Fisher
Sapulpa Community Leader
Majority Leader Oklahoma State Senate

"You don't beat these people, they're still here. They're still active, still participating and still building the community. They've left quite a legacy."

"They were always, always supportive of our Chamber of Commerce. Anything the community needed, you could always count on Liberty's name being associated with it, right down to the football field here…George Collins Stadium."

"The support for United Way was just unbelievable, for an example. We're a big United Way town. You could count on Liberty Glass when it came United Way time. I don't know how they did it. It seemed like every employee of Liberty Glass was a contributor to the United Way. Through their efforts, we easily made our goal."

The Legacy Left Behind…

Bill Berry
American Heritage Bank Chairman

"I think the biggest contribution from that standpoint is United Way. Our [Sapulpa] United Way joined Tulsa, and we were struggling a little bit. Fulton Collins, at the time, and Dave Beyer, organized a program within Liberty Glass to increase participation in the United Way fund. I can remember the first couple of years, not only were their executives each challenged to give $500, but they also challenged their front-line management guys to give the same. This was a big commitment, and they pushed it through. Frankly, we are one of the most successful community United Way programs now, and a part of that is the Key Club program that got its start with Liberty Glass."

"There are a lot of spin-off businesses that are thriving today, because they had contracts to support various Liberty programs, and maintenance and all sorts of things. We've got a great crane operator and a number of tool companies…furnace design engineers and furnace replacements companies."

"My family has been in the banking business here since about 1910. My grandfather is the first member of my family I remember having a business association with the Collins family. They have been good customers, good community supporters, and good friends as long we've been here."

Guy Berry, Sr.

Pete Egan
Sapulpa Community Leader
Author of the book,
"SAPULPA, OK - THE GREATEST CITY IN THE KNOWN WORLD"

"I worked for the city, and we had 80 acres out here on the northeast part of town, and we were going to develop it into a subdivision. And we were going to retain 20 acres for a park. Liberty Glass developed that park, and they spent a lot of time and money. It is called Liberty Park to this day, and it now houses Liberty School. The list goes on and on."

Frank Gierhart
Sapulpa Business and Community Leader
Gabe's Printing

"I just think it's hard to imagine what we would have done without them. We appreciated these people, and they were so generous. They made donations, sponsored people, hired people; it was just a fantastic relationship. They were good people, and I like good people. They were constantly giving back to the community."

Judge Rick Woolery
Judge of District Court
Sapulpa Community Leader
President, Sapulpa Historical Museum

"I think their influence has been so pervasive, and it's hard to imagine people forgetting it. In the mid-1980s I was president of the Chamber, and when we acquired our own building there was considerable financial input from Liberty Glass. We were very grateful for the help on that."

Mike Jeffries
Sapulpa Community Leader
Sapulpa Historical Museum Director

"They supplied a lot of jobs, and were very active in the community, so there was a big sense of partnering. They supported a lot of the non-profits and little league baseball teams and stuff like that for years. They weren't just a business that was in town. They were a part of the community. Their people joined the local clubs and were involved in what was going on in Sapulpa. The yearbooks, they always sponsored the yearbook."

"It's a part of the history of Sapulpa…That way of being involved with the community and of doing business is important, and often gets underappreciated, and the people from Liberty Glass still help, they're still involved, they're still a help with the community. And that's an important legacy."

David Beyer
Accounting Department
Chief Financial Officer
1972-1994

"There was tremendous support there both ways. We [Liberty] never tried to take advantage of that. We always participated a lot in what was going on. There was always a local interest in what was going on, and it was mutual. Even during the strike, we had strong community support, even though part of the community was striking against the company. There was a lot of give and take."

In Sapulpa, many of these gifts continue to benefit young and old alike. Liberty Park still stands, and the football field still beckons fans on Friday nights in the fall.

Over the years, it's been said that at least one person from every family in Sapulpa, no matter what his or her station in life, has benefitted from the work of the George and Jennie Collins Foundation at one time or another. The trust agreement establishing the Foundation states that "all moneys or other property received by the said trustees shall be used exclusively for religious, charitable, scientific, literary or educational purposes or for the prevention of cruelty to children or animals".

Undoubtedly this covers a very broad spectrum. The local Salvation Army Citadel, once considered the finest ever built for a town of Sapulpa's size, was funded almost entirely by the Collins Foundation.

The Foundation was also a major donor to the Centennial Project, "The Guardian of the Plains" Bison statue, Heritage Park, the Tribute piece at Frankoma and the "Y" intersection on New Sapulpa Road. Other donations helped complete the Sapulpa Historical Museum's Waite Phillips Filling Station, and the Fire Museum, which had its grand opening in June of 2013.

Education was always an important focus for the Collins family's philanthropic efforts. George Jr. and his sister Loreine made numerous contributions in that area, both locally and at their father's alma mater, Baker University in Kansas.

Even more impressive is the family's modern-day philanthropy in education. Roger Collins says both he and his brother Fulton felt that strong secondary schools and universities are what help make a community strong.

The Legacy Left Behind...

Roger currently serves as the board chair of Tulsa's Holland Hall, and over the years has continually committed Collins Family Foundation funds to the school. He also supports the University of Tulsa, continuing the legacy of his brother Fulton, although admittedly on a much smaller scale.

Roger knows that Fulton's accomplishments at TU are unprecedented. Ask anyone associated with the University, and they will agree. The impact made by Fulton Collins will be felt for generations to come, and no doubt, the spirit of Liberty Glass will live on through the students at TU. Young people from all over the world who never even heard of Liberty will see the breadth of the company's reach for many years to come.

"Fulton would be so pleased. His dream was fulfilled."

Susie Collins
Wife of Fulton Collins

The LIBERTY Story

The story of Liberty Glass now comes full circle. From the Collins family to the company's employees, the fruits of Liberty's labor now reach far into the future, enriching the lives of many along the way.

Like each and every achievement in the history of Liberty Glass, it was the people that made it all possible, people who toiled side by side, day after day, year after year.

As George Jr. said all those years ago, "I can't do anything, but WE can conquer the world." While Liberty's people may not believe they conquered the world, undoubtedly they realize they made it a much better place.

And this is the legacy Liberty Glass leaves behind.

The Legacy Left Behind...

The Liberty Glass Company by Bill Oldham

The name Liberty Glass and the name Collins are synonymous. You hear one and you think of the other. There's one other name that immediately comes to mind when Liberty Glass is mentioned and that is, Sapulpa, Oklahoma. For Sapulpa would surely not be the town it is had it not been for the vision and development of the glass plant by the Collins family.

Liberty Glass, a privately owned company, competed successfully with the largest glass making corporations in America. It was successful because under the Collins' leadership, they made two things their priority: the quality of their bottles and the way they treated their employees. The quality of Liberty Glass bottles has spoken for itself. They were sought and bought by bottlers all over the U.S.

The manner in which the Collins family treated their employees is also attested to by the employees themselves. It would be impossible to calculate the real impact that Liberty Glass has had on the communities where employees lived.

Liberty Glass always treated their employees fair and paid top wages in the industry.

It is an enduring testimony of thanks to the Collins family that generation after generation, countless families were able to work, raise their families and proudly say, "I work at Liberty Glass."

Above all, it is an enduring testimony of thanks to God for such a gift, provided by a heavenly Father, who knew what we needed before we even ask.

"Every good gift and every perfect gift is from above, coming down from the Father…"
James 1:17 ESV

★ Liberty Glass Company made an early salute to America's Bicentennial with its patriotic booth at the International Soft Drink Exposition, Dallas, Texas, November 17-19, 1975.

★ On the left was an enlargement of the Declaration of Independence. On the right were reproductions of historic shrines of the Revolutionary War: Valley Forge, Yorktown Battlefield, The Old North Church, Independence Hall, Mount Vernon, and Monticello.

Liberty Glass Company
SAPULPA, OKLAHOMA

Addendum One

Transportation was an integral part of the Liberty Glass operation. Moving raw materials into the plant and finished products out were costly endeavors. Two companies, Tulsa - Sapulpa Union Railway and Red Ball Trucking, also owned by the Collins family, helped Liberty effectively meet its substantial transportation needs.

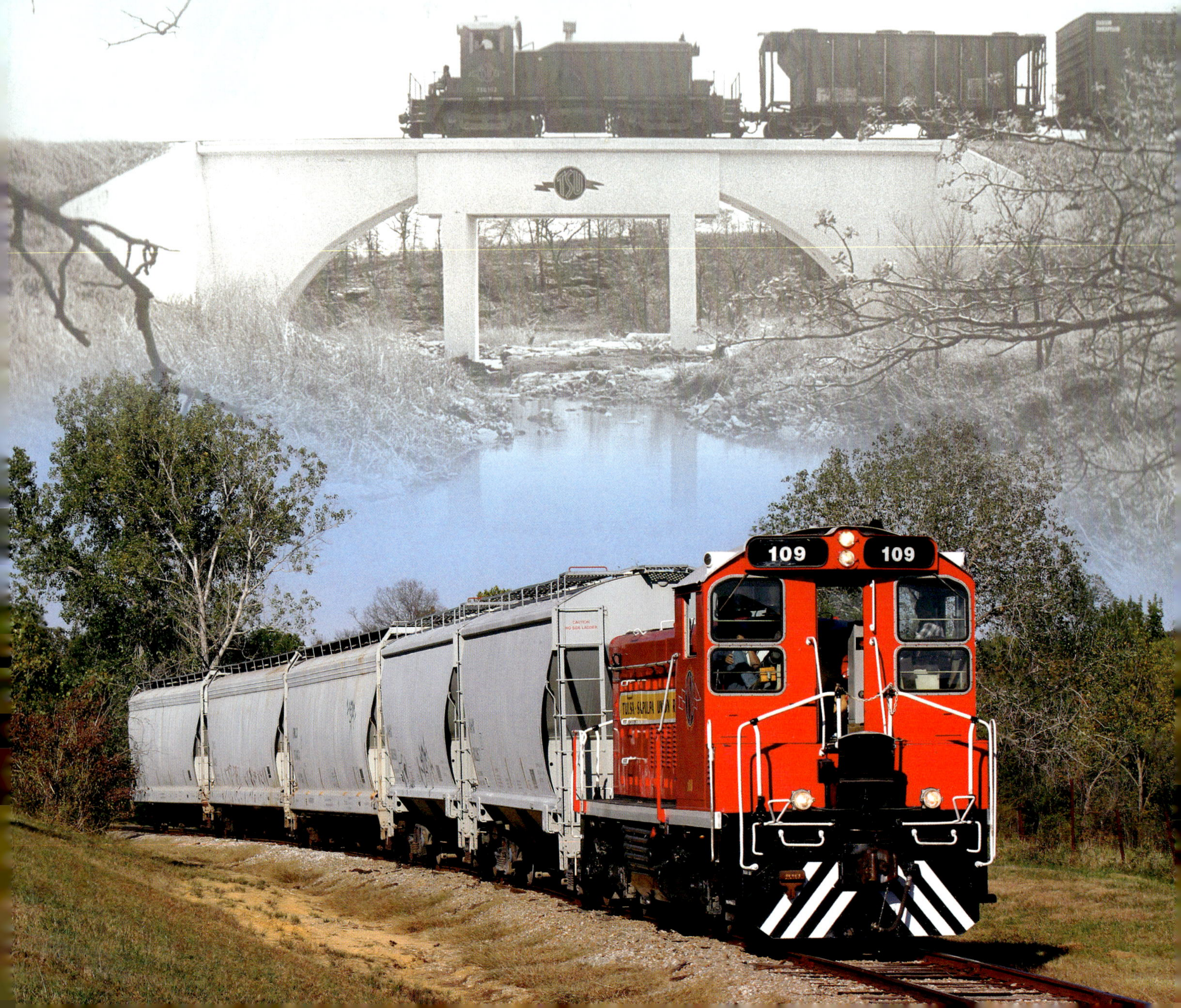

The Tulsa-Sapulpa Union Railway Co. (TSU), a small Oklahoma short-line railway operating between Sapulpa and Tulsa, played an important role in the history of Liberty Glass. In 1934 the rail line was in receivership and was purchased by George F. Collins Sr.

This was a sensible solution for transporting raw materials needed to manufacture glass products into the plant. After George's purchase, the railway became a freight-only operation and passenger services were no longer available. Not surprisingly, Liberty Glass quickly became one of the rail line's biggest customers.

The roots of TSU can be traced going all the way back to statehood in 1907, the year Sapulpa was also incorporated. The railway operated as an inter-urban streetcar line using trolley cars around Sapulpa. The line was later extended from Sapulpa to the newly discovered oil fields at Kiefer and Glenpool.

This was at an exciting time in Oklahoma history as the oil industry was coming of age. The line provided transportation for workers and business people alike in these growing oilfields and communities.

Despite the prosperity in the area, the line underwent bankruptcy and reorganization, and in 1917 was incorporated as the Sapulpa Electric Inter-Urban Railway. This same year the railway was extended north to connect with the Oklahoma Union Railway out of Tulsa. A number of famous people have ties to the Inter-Urban such as J.S. Cosden, E.F. Sinclair and Tom Slick, all of whom were making their marks in the oil boom.

Tulsa-Sapulpa Union Railway

After undergoing several name changes along the way, the Tulsa-Sapulpa Union Railway was the final name given to the company in 1943 under George Collins Jr.'s leadership. Keeping in line with Liberty's commitment to patriotism, two of the motor cars were repainted red, white and blue and emblazoned with an appeal to "Buy War Bonds." Thanks to growing revenues at this time, money was spent to upgrade the railway.

In the late 1950s the line fought a prolonged and sometimes acrimonious battle with the state highway department, which wanted to cross the TSU right of way with a new freeway. The highway department felt that total abandonment would be cheaper than building a single freeway overpass, and pointed out that the main line of the Frisco went right past the Liberty Glass Plant. TSU held its ground and the railway stayed in business.

David Beyer
Liberty Accounting Department and CFO
1972-1994
Current TSU President

"TSU's primary importance was connecting freight service with two major railroads - initially, the Frisco (Sapulpa) and the Missouri Pacific (West Tulsa), now the Burlington Northern and the Union Pacific, respectively. These two connections provided competitive pricing for raw materials such as silica, sand, limestone and soda ash, which, during the 1990s, was 10 carloads daily. Periodically, Liberty also shipped finished product by rail. Competitive pricing was very important to Liberty's success as a one plant operation, because our competitors had multiple plants with greater purchasing power. The close working relationship between the two companies helped ensure that Liberty Glass always had an adequate supply of raw materials to keep the plant operating 24/7. The two connections also provided alternate routes for raw materials in the event service was interrupted with one of the major carriers."

Like Liberty Glass, TSU had many loyal and long-term employees. Lonny Simonds began working at the company in January of 1971 and didn't leave until 40 years later in 2011. Lonny started at TSU doing track work, a difficult job during Oklahoma's long, hot summers and cold wet winters, especially if a train got derailed.

Lonny Simonds
TSU Supervisor of Locomotive Engineers
1971-2011

"It wasn't good."

"In the wintertime, it didn't matter whether it was snow or wet or anything else, you were under there trying to get back up."

"Sometimes we'd have to call a crane out and that wasn't good."

Tulsa-Sapulpa Union Railway

Lonny also recalls TSU actually moving railroad cars into the Liberty plant each morning. The glass facility featured a track that ran right through the middle of the plant.

Lonny Simonds
TSU Supervisor of Locomotive Engineers
1971-2011

"They were putting three to four cars in the glass plant in the morning."

"Sometimes those cars didn't have very good brakes, and they'd get away from you and roll out to the highway."

Russell Crosby, another veteran TSU employee, came to the company right out of Northeastern State University in 1974, and remains there today. He, too, remembers all the years of trying to keep the track in good operating condition.

Russell Crosby
TSU Vice President/General Manager
1974-Today

"Everything was done the old fashioned way. It would be hot out there laying track."

"The track is always sinking... moving around."

"Short lines all have their own personality. You've got all sizes of rail in there."

"Heat causes it to expand and the cold causes it to contract. You're always having to deal with that track. Trying to keep where you could stay on it and not being off on the ground."

"Snakes made for excitement."

Russell Crosby started at TSU in accounting and today serves as Vice President and General Manager, but over the years he recalls functioning in a variety of jobs.

"You never knew what you were going to be doing, which sort of took the boredom out of it."

Russell also remembers the family atmosphere that made TSU a great place to work, and feels that is why many of the employees remained so loyal to the company.

"I don't think there's ever been a time in the history of TSU when there weren't at least two brothers working there at all times. It was very family oriented."

Tulsa-Sapulpa Union Railway

This article from the 1958 Tulsa Tribune confirms Russell's observation on family and TSU.

The Tulsa Tribune

Sapulpa Union A "Family Affair"
Robbins Brothers Keep Trains Rolling
Tulsa Tribune, 1958

In any analysis of what makes the Tulsa-Sapulpa Union Railway go, the Robbins brothers of Sapulpa must be ranked right along with the trolley cable that powers the 13-mile line.

Of the railroad's 10 train and section workers, five are Robbins. J. Earnest, a small, wiry man of 66, is a head trainman (engineer). Ben 43, is a crew member. Houston, 51, and Bill, 58, work as needed as extra train hands and on the section, and George, 55, is a full-time section worker.

Earnest has been jockeying trolley cars and electric locomotives since 1913, when he started with the Sapulpa Electric Interurban, which served Sapulpa proper, and shuttled to Kiefer.

While he was overseas in World War I, the line was bought by Tulsa street railway interests and linked with the Tulsa system. Later the line was extended southward to Mounds, and Earnest went the full route from Mounds to the fairgrounds in Tulsa.

Earnest broke the railroading ice for himself and his four brothers because the right-of-way to Mounds ran through his father's farm south of Sapulpa.

"I knew all the boys that worked for the line, and they asked me to quit the farm and come to work for them," he said.

Ben went to work in 1935-"when jobs weren't too easy to get"- and was followed within a few months by Houston. Bill signed up with the "Sapulpa Union," as home folks call the road, in 1937, and George joined the ranks five years ago.

The five have a total of 117 years with the road, minus time out for Earnest's, Ben's and Houston's military service. And at one time a sixth brother, Jack, was on the payroll for a short time.

The Sapulpa Union now is owned by the George F. Collins family, which also has the Liberty Glass Company in Sapulpa. About 90 per of the car loadings consists of silica sand, limestone, soda ash, and other raw materials for the glass firm and the products of the company when they are moved from Sapulpa to Tulsa to be picked up by long lines.

Rolling stock consists of two locomotives, a trolley car that also can pull loads, five box cars, and a work car.

The work unit is a flat car. On it is a wooden tower that enables section men to repair and maintain the 600-volt direct current overhead line.

SECTION THREE
PAGE FORTY-ONE
WEDNESDAY, MAY 7, 1958

The Tuls

THE RAILROADIN' ROBBINSES — The five Robbins brothers of Sapulpa make up half of the train and section personnel of the Tulsa-Sapulpa Union Railway Co: Left to right are J. Earnest, head trainman who has been with the line since 1913; Ben, a train crewman; Houston and Bill, who double as train and section hands, as needed, and George, a section worker. The brothers' service with the road aggregates 117 years. (Tribune Staff Photo)

Sapulpa Union a 'Family Affair'

Robbins Brothers Keep Trains Rolling

Earnest, Ben and their fellow crewmen make two round trips daily, except Sunday, leaving Sapulpa between 9 and 10 in the morning, returning from West Tulsa terminal at noon, and making an afternoon run between 1 and 4.

They haul only freight, passenger service having been discontinued in the early 1930's.

Engineer Earnest has had one wreck and back in 1938 or '39 – he wasn't exactly sure of the year – the trains didn't run for two days when Polecat Creek went out of its banks north of Sapulpa and was five or six feet over the tracks.

The wreck was a head-on collision of two large interurban cars near the old Crystal City Park in 1923. Earnest's accident report; "The other one ran into me."

All the Robbins are members of the Brotherhood of Railroad Trainmen West Tulsa Local 619.

At 66, Earnest has been eligible for retirement for more than a year. He has five children, all grown, and seven grandchildren, but there's no indication he won't continue to climb into his cab each morning and ease his engine toward West Tulsa. Says he: "I like to run 'em."

Russell Crosby
TSU
Vice President/General Manager
1974-Today

"The TSU Railway has a wonderful history. Unlike most short line railroads in the state, it is not a spin-off of a branch line of one of the major class-one rail carriers, such as the BNSF or Union Pacific. TSU operates on the original right of way from Sapulpa to Tulsa that was used by the trolley system. The railway operated with electric overhead lines until 1960. It now operates with four 1200 horsepower diesel electric Electro-Motive Division switch locomotives. These units are about 60 years old, but give very dependable service."

Tulsa-Sapulpa Union Railway

Another fond memory for many of those associated with TSU over the years is the Murray Hill, a 1929 Pullman business car, owned by TSU and George Collins Jr. Russell Crosby says this car was one of Mr. Collins' most prized possessions.

Russell Crosby
TSU Vice President/General Manager
1974-Today

"Mr. Collins purchased the Murray Hill in the early 70s, probably in 1972 or 1973. I was impressed that he was the sole owner of his own little railroad and had his own business car. Not many folks in the United States can say they own their own operating railroad lock, stock and barrel.

The car was stored at the TSU railway shops off Dewey Street in Sapulpa. It was only operated on the railway for special occasions. Those occasions would usually be a grand opening for a new customer who had settled in TSU's Parthenia Industrial District, or other occasions, such as a special outing hosted by the Collins family for their family and friends.

TSU Railway passes were issued to each passenger riding aboard the Murray Hill on TSU's Buffalo route. It was issued as a souvenir of their time aboard the TSU. As it turned out, the TSU Railway now operates within a block of Sapulpa's State Centennial project, "THE GUARDIAN OF THE PLAINS," a twice life sized statue of the American bison. The George F. Collins Jr. Foundation and the George and Jennie Collins Foundation were major financial contributors to this Community project.

The Pullman was named the Murray Hill, a name it was given when it was originally built. It was a beautiful rail passenger car. The car was about 85 feet long and was built in 1929 by the Pullman Company. It had six single bedrooms, a buffet-type kitchen, and, at the end of the car, was a sunroom or solarium.

J.E. Williams, son-in-law of Thelis Lucas, who was a long term employee at TSU, recalls that the Murray Hill came to TSU in pretty rough shape. Thelis dismantled the interior, and restored the car inside and out, which included new paint and fixtures. He was able to eventually restore the car to its original grandeur.

The car was painted in the traditional Pullman green color for the exterior, with the top painted a rusty red color. The car had the TSU logos hand painted on each end. The name of the railway was also hand painted on each side of the car in gold leaf. This was very striking to say the least. The interior was just like walking back in time on the old railroads. The car had most of the original artifacts such as linens, coats, china, furniture and numerous other items still with it.

The car was an operating challenge each time we took it out. It was so long, it made it difficult to operate on tight curves over certain areas on the railway without the fear of a possible derailment.

From published history on the internet, the Murray Hill was operated on the New York and New Haven and Hartford railroad, which was known as the New Haven Railroad. It ran from Boston, through New York, to Washington, D.C. until 1954. While we are not sure of its use from the latter '50s to the time of purchase by George F. Collins Jr., it appears that Mr. Collins purchased the car directly from the New Haven Railroad.

The car was given to the Sunbelt Historical Railroad Trust sometime in the mid-'80s after Mr. Collins passed away. It then had quite a rough existence being stored on the Sand Springs Railway rail sidings, with hopes that the group could restore it to passenger service in the Tulsa area.

Unfortunately that never happened. Vandals took their toll with a fire set in one end of the car, some windows were broken and artifacts were stolen. Paint started peeling, and she was a pretty sad looking lady. It was very near being cut-up when, in 2011, the Route 66 Village group saved her and gave her renewed life with a new paint job and lettering and a new home for her to be displayed at the Route 66 Village.

The Murray Hill is now back in her glory. I suspect that Mr. Collins looks down with pleasure knowing one of his favorite pieces of the TSU railroad remains intact and honored.

Incidentally, as railroad trivia, the move of this car and steam locomotive was the only time that steam-powered locomotive equipment was ever operated over the rails of the TSU. The Murray Hill is still in the process of being completely restored so that people can go through her and see what passenger travel was like in the good old days.

Vintage railroad cars on display in west Tulsa

BY KEVIN CANFIELD
World Staff Writer

Charles DeVilbiss, 83, watched three vintage railroad cars travel 2.5 miles through west Tulsa on Sunday morning and was transported back in time 65 years.

He has a special attachment to one of the cars — the 1942 blue-and-silver Frisco 4500. The 500,000-pound steam locomotive was nearly new when De-Vilbiss used to ride it while local telegraph

Frisco 1157 caboose, built in the 1930s or 1940s as a boxcar from a storage site inside Holl Corp. refinery west along rai road tracks on the southeast si of Southwest Boulevard.

Then, using 300 feet of te porary track laid Saturday, railroad cars were pushed no across Southwest Boulevard into Route 66 Village.

"It's a virus you get when are very young," DeVilbiss of his love of trains. "It is by your grandfather. You get over it. There is no k cure."

Time will tell how Ca 10, handles his t he can surely , Ken Mc im.

Through the years the TSU rail line played an important role not only in Sapulpa, but in surrounding communities as well. When nearby Jenks celebrated its 100th Anniversary in 2005, TSU joined in the festivities since Jenks had an important presence in the railway's daily operations.

In honor of the town's celebration, TSU chose to repaint one of its engines in a burgundy color and renumber the engine as well. The burgundy was chosen to match Jenks' school colors and the new engine number marked the centennial date.

When the engine rolled by the high school during homecoming week, even the whistle it sounded seem to say "Go Trojans." Some TSU employees later admitted this was not exactly an easy decision as Sapulpa and Jenks had long been rivals in high school football. But as we have learned, Liberty's legacy put a strong emphasis on community, and Jenks was part of the community served by TSU.

Today the rail line continues to operate, still serving industry between Sapulpa and Tulsa, including the St. Gobain Glass Plant, Prescor, Greenbay Packaging, Atlantis Plastics, CG Martin Company and Technotherm.

The railway also operates trackage between Tulsa and Jenks on behalf of the Union Pacific Railroad serving Holly Oil Refinery, Kentube, Word Industries and Kimberly Clark. TSU has a direct connection with the Union Pacific in Tulsa and Burlington Northern Santa Fe railroad in Sapulpa, serving customers in the Tulsa Metropolitan area.

Mike Averill of The Tulsa World gave us a brief glimpse into TSU's more recent operations in this article, published in 2006.

TULSA WORLD, Wednesday, June 28, 2006
Re-published with permission of The Tulsa World

Working the tracks
Railway teams continue tradition on Sapulpa's short-line system
By Mike Averill
World Staff Writer

The 10-to 12-hour days can be grueling, monotonous and grinding. Most of the work is hooking and unhooking train cars and rearranging them so they'll be in the right order for delivery. Sure there are beautiful days, but this is Oklahoma.

Much of the work is done in blistering heat with no shade, a spring rain too fierce to call a shower or freezing temperatures with a biting wind. This is the life of a railroad worker at the Tulsa-Sapulpa Union Railway.

TSU isn't one of the large transcontinental railways that coasts at 50 miles per hour from location to location. It's a short-line railway, which connects smaller customers and communities to the larger railways.

So what is it that attracts the short-line workers?

"It's like the last glimpse into something old," said Terry Tucker, engineer and switchman. "It's one of the few things that hasn't changed."

TSU operates about 23 miles of track between Sapulpa and Tulsa and Jenks. It's one of the oldest operating railways in the state. Its origins date back to 1907.

The railway handles about 7,500 cars a year, each carrying approximately 100 tons.

"That might not sound like a lot, but when you see the operation, there's a lot of coupling and uncoupling, and it takes a lot of time," said Russell Crosby, vice president and general manager.

The railway workers operate in three-man teams, with one person controlling the engine with the other two on the ground. Because the engineer cannot see the two switchmen, trust and communication are key.

"You have to be able to trust what your fellow employee tells you to do and trust that it is safe," Crosby said.

Trust is one reason the industry is so close knit, with many family members and friends working together.

"You're spending 10 to 12 hours a day together," Tucker said. "It's in a pretty tight space, so you want to find someone you can get along with."

There are about 65 railroad crossings along the TSU line, and impatient drivers are always a concern. "That's just the environment we operate in," Crosby said. "There are people, vehicles and pedestrians around us all the time. We never have a clear road to work with. People tend to think we can stop faster than we can. All this equipment is big and unforgiving, and things can get real bad, real fast."

TSU is one of 16 short-lines in Oklahoma. According to the American Short Line and Regional Railroad Association, in 1980 there were 190 short lines in the country operating on 8,000 miles of track. Now there are more than 500 short lines operating nearly 50,000 miles of track, or 30 percent of the national railway system.

"Railroads are a pretty exciting piece of America," Crosby said.

As time and TSU roll on, much has changed, but today the line still remains with the Collins family. Owned by the George F. Collins Jr. Trust, dated 1969. George's younger son Roger continues to lead the company, and even though the railway has many new customers, it will best be remembered as the line that helped launch Liberty Glass to the top of its industry.

Red Ball Trucking was another Collins family enterprise, designed to aid in the transportation needs of Liberty Glass. George Collins Jr., who made the purchase, felt it quickly gave Liberty the ability to be more responsive to its customers' needs.

Pete Egan's book "SAPULPA, OK - THE GREATEST CITY IN THE KNOWN WORLD".

"George F. Collins bought part of the Red Ball Transfer and Storage Company, owned by R.W. Wallace. Collins bought several trucks and the license to haul products such as glass, sugar, boxes and general commodities. Wallace's company retained two trucks and the right to haul and store furniture in a seven-state area. Wallace would keep the same name and would stay at 611 South Main. Collins' company would be named Red Ball, Inc., located at the old refinery and operated by Berry Rea."

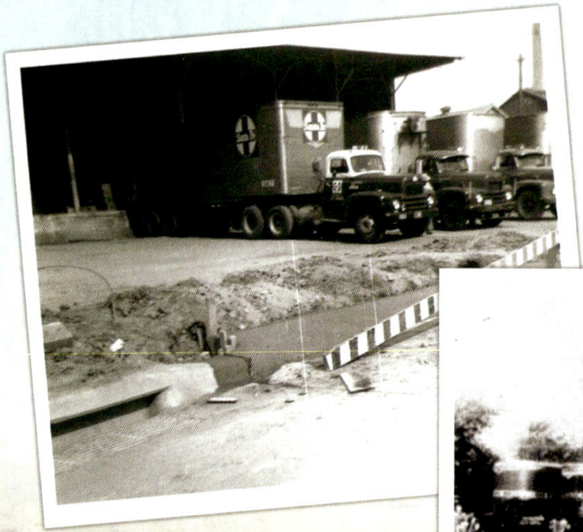

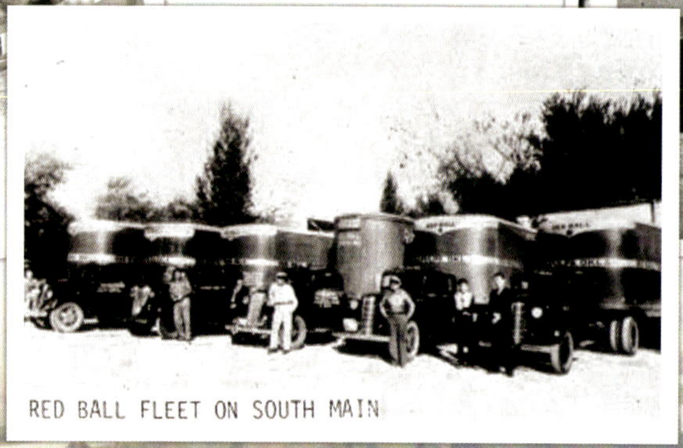

RED BALL FLEET ON SOUTH MAIN

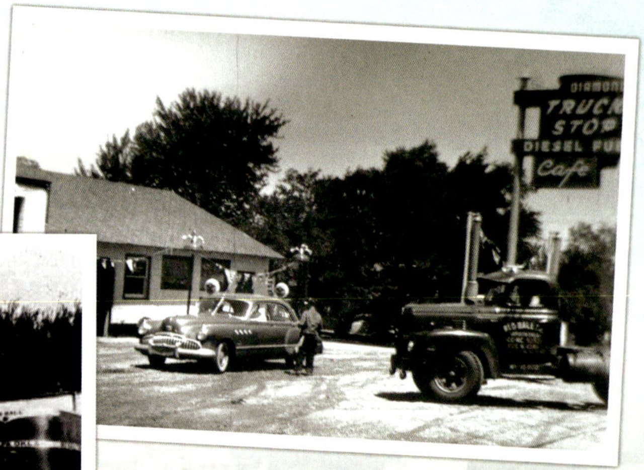

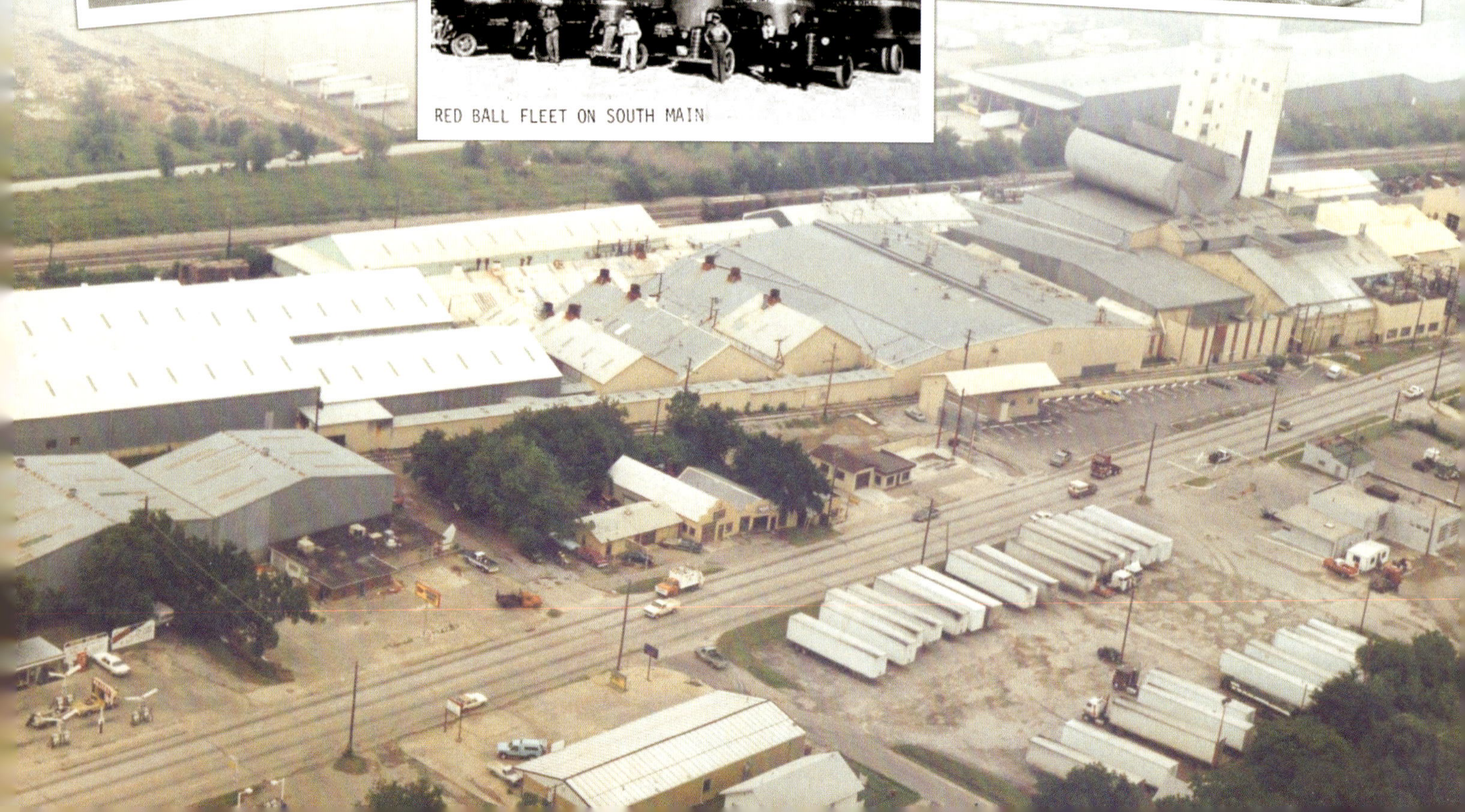

LG

Roger Collins
Son of George Collins Jr.
Management
1977-1981

"Before de-regulation in the trucking industry, he [George Jr.] needed a way to get Liberty Glass Company's bottles to its customers in a timely and cost-effective manner."

"Frank Burzio and then Ed Gosvener had turns running Red Ball. George Summers was Vice President of Sales. After de-regulation Ed, with George's help, was challenged to grow Red Ball's customer base. Initially they were charged with finding return freight near Liberty's customers he was delivering to. As I recall, they were able to grow the company to about 100 trucks with their expanded business base."

"Red Ball was a union carrier and the family trust that owned it finally concluded that our union contract was never going to permit us to operate it at more than a break-even (competing more and more with non-union carriers). So we elected to shut it down. When we did that George Summers, VP of Sales, came to me and said that he was interested in starting a new carrier that could benefit from his relationships with Red Ball's customers, but he wanted to do it with independent contractors as drivers rather than union drivers. But he lacked the financial capital to make it work. Several years prior to that I had purchased another trucking company in Fort Worth, Texas, with a group of venture capitalists. Through that acquisition I had gained knowledge on how profitable trucking companies are run. So I agreed to back George in starting up a new carrier, under the condition that no other employees from Red Ball came with the deal. I did not want the union to see this as a successor carrier, and have any claim in that regard. So with that, he started Interstate Express, and it was profitable in its first year of operation. Several years later, George retired and I merged Interstate with a couple of other trucking companies that I had also invested in."

Addendum Two
The Collins Building

For many years, the Collins Building in downtown Sapulpa housed Liberty employees who did not work at the plant. This included company executives and the administrative staff, plus the IT, Accounting and Sales departments.

With stately columns reaching into the sky, the building was originally a Masonic Temple. Built in 1925, the structure next became the home for Liberty when it was purchased by George F. Collins Jr. in 1942. The Masonic Lodge failed to pay off its bonds on the building, and it eventually went into receivership.

R. Bruce Ryan
Accounting Department
Plant Accountant, Assistant Controller, Controller
1982-1992

"When I interviewed and it was at the Collins Building, I remember thinking this is a pretty impressive office building for a one-plant glass company. That stuck in my mind."

Living History
Collins Building Restored to Original State

Liberty Glass Company
SAPULPA, OKLAHOMA

Even though the building was indeed impressive, having multiple locations for Liberty had been cumbersome at best. When Gary Oyler first came to the company, it was his responsibility to make up for the inefficiency this caused.

Gary Oyler
Service, Inventory, Payroll
1978-1994

"I started out in the service department. I ran the trips out to the factory with the mail back and forth [from the Collins Building]. And shipped the samples out…twice a day. You took the mail to TSU, and of course the shipments and stuff went to Red Ball."

"All the shipping orders went out that way. If they had a hot item that needed to ship right away they'd telex the order. That was before fax machines and all that stuff."

"You'd take inter-office mail or whatever to the Collins Building, and you'd pick up what mail was coming out. Or if you had some kind of sample that needed to go out, you'd go pick that up out at the factory and take it to the Collins."

"Some of what you took out to the factory was scheduling changes or requests for production runs. When they'd get enough together to run say Pepsi or Coke for enough customers, they would have a scheduling change. They'd try to plan it out ahead."

The Collins Building

Shortly after Fulton Collins took over leadership of the company, one of the first things he did was move everyone out of the Collins Building. He felt having Liberty split between two locations did not suit his company's best interests. With the goal of forming a more cohesive, efficient company, Fulton transferred all the employees out to the plant.

| Susie Collins
Wife of Fulton Collins | *"Fulton said, 'I need to move out of this building and be at the plant'. He would walk the plant twice a day. He felt it was so important to be at the plant and be seen. He was a hands-on leader."* |

Most employees agreed this was a good move, as not only did having one location mean a more efficient company, it also promoted camaraderie among the various departments.

| Linda Campbell
Sales Department Receptionist | *"I thought it was exciting. I hated to leave the building itself. But it was better for all of us to be together… you could get things done faster."* |

Some years after Liberty left the Collins Building, it was acquired by the Creek County Industrial Authority for $218,000, and in 1989 was donated to the county. Today the county commissioner, as well as the county clerk, treasurer and assessor staffs are housed in the structure.

The beautiful building remains one of Creek County's most prominent architectural treasures, and most in Sapulpa say even though Liberty is long gone, the building will always be referred to as the Collins Building.

Presenting the ECONOTAINER
The Square Milk Bottle

Strengthen your mind by completing the course of study of the Sapulpa High School.
Strengthen your body by drinking milk bottled and delivered in Liberty Bottles.

They Satisfy

Liberty Glass Company
Sapulpa, Oklahoma

A Modern Design From An Old Style!

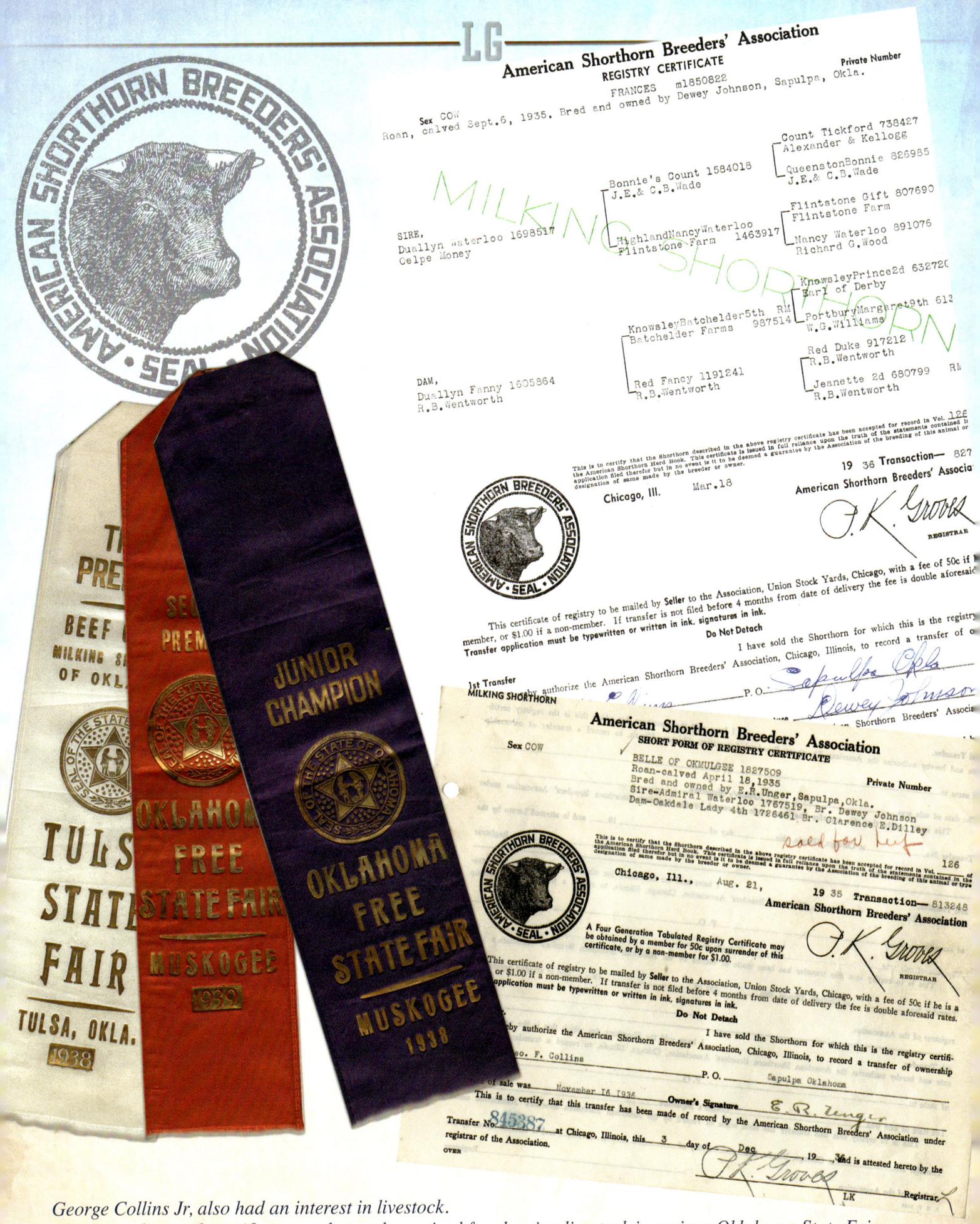

*George Collins Jr, also had an interest in livestock.
Above, are livestock certificates and awards received for showing livestock in various Oklahoma State Fairs.*

Acknowledgements
Thank you

We would like to thank the many Liberty Glass employees and Sapulpa community leaders who shared their memories and stories. Their contributions enabled us to provide readers with a vivid description of the many people and events that made up the history of Liberty Glass.

We wish to thank:

Lonny Simonds	Mike Tyler	Margaret Ann Fuller
Russell Crosby	Bill Berry	Kathy Wilson
Kitty Hunt	Pete Egan	Bruce Ryan
Doris Yocham	David Beyer	Mike Wille
Bill Oldham	Jim Bolin	Frank Gierhart
Joyce Steavenson	Rick Woolery	Bart Bartlett
Jackie Robertson	Mike Jeffries	Robert Lorton
Catherine Williams	Robert Hall	John Conway
Velma Littlefield	Vickie Beyer	Susie Collins
Gary Oyler	David Bennett	Steadman Upham
Bob Hill	Roger Collins	Beverley Collins Ward
Tom Syrles	Linda Campbell	Carolyn Collins
Terry Kelly	Wills Young	Suzanne Collins Yonkers
Glenn Nix	Alene Giese	Chrissy Collins Mantzuranis
Johnny Brison	David Block	Fulton Collins IV
Ted Fisher	David Fieker	

Acknowledgements
Thank you

This publication would not have been possible without all of those who provided photographs and other memorabilia showcasing the history of Liberty Glass. Their valuable contributions allowed us to preserve and illustrate the special story of Liberty Glass.

Our deepest appreciation and sincere thanks to:

Trina Lucas	Charles R. H. Myers
J.E. Williams	Gary Oyler
Thelis & Betty Lucas	Roger Collins
Tom Syrles	Susie Collins
Bill Oldham	Beverley Collins Ward
Lonny Simonds	John Brock
Russell Crosby	Hazel Boaz
Belinda Crosby	Ian Danziger, Danziger Photography
Brean Crosby Fowler	Kayla Acebo, University of Tulsa
Joyce Steavenson	Mike Palmieri
David Beyer	Blair Koositra
Glenn Nix	Sapulpa Historical Society
Robert Hall	Sapulpa Public Library
Chief Eaton	The Daily Oklahoman
Linda Campbell	Sapulpa Daily Herald
Margaret Ann Fuller